The Ultimate Stress Handbook for Women

Ursula Markham is a practising hypnotherapist. In addition to running her own successful clinic, she gives lectures and conducts workshops and seminars in Britain and abroad. She has appeared frequently on radio and television, and is Principal of the Hypnothink Foundation, which is responsible for the training of hypnotherapists and counsellors to professional levels.

by the same author

The Ultimate Stress Handbook for Women

URSULA MARKHAM

ELEMENT
Shaftesbury, Dorset • Rockport,
Massachusetts • Brisbane, Queensland

© Element Books Limited 1997
Text © Ursula Markham 1997

First published in Great Britain in 1997 by
Element Books Limited
Shaftesbury, Dorset SP7 8BP

Published in the USA in 1997 by
Element Books, Inc.
PO Box 830, Rockport, MA 01966

Published in Australia in 1997 by
Element Books Limited
for Jacaranda Wiley Limited
33 Park Road, Milton, Brisbane 4064

Cover design by Slatter-Anderson
Page design by Roger Lightfoot
Typeset by WestKey Limited, Falmouth, Cornwall
Printed and bound in Great Britain by Creative Print and Design
(Wales), Ebbw Vale.

British Library Cataloguing in Publication data available

Library of Congress Cataloging in Publication data available

ISBN 1-85230-857-5

To my mother and the women whose
friendship I treasure

*The spirit of self-help is the root of all genuine
growth in the individual*

Samuel Smiles, 1812–1904

Contents

Introduction

I wonder what your thoughts were as you looked at the title of this book. Did you feel that I was being sexist or did it appear that I was implying that men did not suffer from stress?

Neither of these is true. I am not an ardent feminist and of course I know that men suffer from stress. It is just that there are so many extra stress-inducing factors in the lives of women.

Whether she is young or old, working outside the home or looking after a family, involved in a relationship or alone, a woman has all the 20th-century stress-related problems that a man has . . . and then some!

This book is designed to help you. It cannot eliminate all the stressful situations in your life – although the techniques contained here can help you to minimize many of them. What it can do is ensure that you never again have to suffer physically, mentally or emotionally because of those stressful situations.

The methods described have been well tried and tested during the 17 years I have been in practice as a hypnotherapist and counsellor. They work. I know they work. And you will see them work when you read the case histories – all of which are taken from my own files, with only the names changed.

If these methods work for other women, they can work for you. You can change your life for the better – starting now.

Chapter One

Becoming Aware

I'd like you to make me a promise. Promise me that you'll never try to eliminate stress from your life.

Does that seem a strange request to make when all around us there is so much talk of stress and its harmful effects? Did you begin to read this book in the first place because you are desperately trying to rid yourself of the problems caused by stress? You may have thought this to be so but what you are really trying to do is eliminate *excess* stress from your life.

There is a great difference between stress and excess stress. A certain amount of stress is good for us; in fact it is essential if we are to be the active, creative women we would wish to be – women who are able to face the challenges and withstand the pressures of life. The right amount of stress helps us to think on our feet, come up with innovative ideas and cope with emergencies.

Excess stress, however, is quite another matter. Excess stress, particularly over a prolonged period, is the enemy. Excess stress saps our energy, drains us emotionally and leaves us vulnerable to any number of physical and psychological problems.

If you are to achieve the right sort of balance in your life, you need to know several things.

- how to recognize that you are suffering from excess stress;
- instant stress-relief techniques to deal with the immediate situation;

- how to identify your personal stressors and to prepare for them so that they do not have their usual effect;
- how to cope when circumstances create unavoidable stressful situations;
- how to recover from the effects of excess stress and how to control it in the future;
- where to find outside help should you need it.

What is stress?

Let's look at what happens to you physically when you are in a highly stressful situation.

A series of changes occurs in your body within a short space of time:

- the demand for oxygen increases;
- heart and pulse rate increase;
- muscles tense and you begin to sweat;
- blood pressure rises;
- extra adrenalin is produced.

These changes occur in both men and women but the last one – the increase in adrenalin production – has a special significance for women. The more adrenalin your body is in the process of producing, the less you produce of essential female hormones. You only have to look at the miserable cycle endured by so many women just before or upon the start of their periods to see the effect this can have. Knowledge that it is 'that time of the month', with all its attendant discomforts, causes tension. Tension (stress) induces an excess of adrenalin production; the extra adrenalin causes a reduction in the production of female hormones and therefore the period itself is even more difficult (physically and/or emotionally). This in turn causes even more tension the following month.

Of course this situation does not affect every woman. There are those who appear to sail unconcernedly through their monthly cycle. But it is easy to see how, once the syndrome begins, it soon becomes self-perpetuating unless something positive is done to break the pattern.

Recognizing excess stress

Because excess stress has a habit of creeping up almost unnoticed, you might not even be aware that you are suffering from its effects. Oh, you might know that you've been getting more headaches than usual or that lately you have been finding it difficult to sleep at night. Others might complain that you are becoming less efficient or more irritable and – even if you vehemently deny it – you probably know in your heart that they are right.

The difficulty arises because you may well not consider these changes as symptoms of excess stress. After all, everyone has headaches, don't they? And if you don't realize that a problem exists, there is little hope of your doing anything to overcome it.

So before we go any further, take a look at the list of possible symptoms that follows and see which (if any) apply to you. Remember to tick only those which occur regularly or which are increasing either in number or severity. The occasional sleepless night or bout of indigestion doesn't count.

Physical symptoms

headaches	increased alcohol
tired eyes	consumption
insomnia	fatigue
tiredness on waking	restlessness
constipation	dizziness or nausea
sexual problems	frequent crying
overeating	high blood pressure

aching muscles
chest pains
nightmares
PMT
diarrhoea
indigestion
lack of appetite

increased smoking
breathing difficulties
nervous habits
feelings of panic
increased irritability
racing heart/seeming to miss
   a beat

Mental/emotional symptoms

apathy
difficulty in concentrating
fears/phobias
inability to cope
fears about future
poor self-esteem
inability to make
   decisions
general anxiety

poor memory
poor communication with
   others
no sense of humour
inability to display emotion
guilt about past
feelings of failure
suppressed anger
feeling misunderstood

If you are experiencing five or more of the symptoms in each of the above lists more often than usual, or if they occur frequently in your life, you are probably suffering from excess stress.

(By the way, why not refer back to these lists in a month or two's time when you have had a chance to put some of the ideas in this book into practice? I think you'll be pleasantly surprised at the reduced number of symptoms which apply to you.)

Why excess stress causes these symptoms

When excess stress creates the physical changes in your body you become like a pressure cooker with an enormous build up of internal 'steam'. You'll know that every pressure cooker has a small lever or button somewhere which, when activated, allows the steam to escape – thus avoiding an explosion! Just like the pressure cooker, you need to find a way of releasing the 'steam' if it is not to cause a physical or psychological 'explosion' within you.

But perhaps you are someone who doesn't notice that this pressure is building up within you until it is too late and you are already suffering from its detrimental effects. If that could be the case, try and get into the habit over the next seven to ten days of stopping at intervals during the day and taking note of a few possible early-warning signals. (And before you say that you are so busy that you don't have the time to stop for anything at all, let me say that, for one thing, this need not take more than three or four minutes and, for another, such self-awareness might well end up saving you both time and temper in the long run.)

When you do stop, take note of the following things.

- Is your jaw clenched tightly closed?
- Are your temples beginning to throb?
- Do your shoulders ache?
- Are you frowning?
- Do you feel irritable or flustered?

If you can answer 'yes' to any of the above, then tension is already building up and you should do something about it before it really takes hold.

Now I realize that, if you are in the middle of a hectic day – whether at home or at your place of work – this is not the time to take 20 minutes to practise a deep relaxation routine. But even if you can spare no more than two minutes, you can put 'instant stress release' into action.

Instant stress release

At the first possible moment, stop what you are doing. Stand up, stretching your spine without becoming too rigid. Shake your shoulders up and down and, when you stop, make sure that they are relaxed and lowered rather than tensed and up by your ears. Open and close your mouth a couple of times – as though you are yawning – to relax your jaw. Now close your eyes and take two deep breaths, breathing from your diaphragm rather than your upper chest.

That may be all you have time to do at that moment. But it will be enough to release the tension from your body and ensure that any stress you are undergoing is not doing you any harm.

Either immediately or as soon as possible afterwards, depending upon how much time you have and what you are doing, try and work out what it was that caused you to feel so tense. Is there some major worry playing on your mind or was it just a series of petty annoyances?

If you have a serious problem in your life at the moment, no one is going to suggest that you will not feel stressed or that you can make yourself forget about it. If someone in your family is seriously ill, if you have just been made redundant, if a relationship is coming to an end, if there is a danger that your business could fail or your house be repossessed, of course you are going to be anxious and feel concerned. It is quite understandable that excess stress will build up, but if you allow it to take hold so that you suffer physically or emotionally, ask yourself a couple of questions. Firstly, will all the worry in the world improve the situation? I think not. You are either in a position where you can do something about what is happening or it is beyond your control. If the former, you are less likely to act rationally and in the best interests of yourself and others if you are so tense that you cannot think straight. If the situation is one which you cannot control, of course you will still worry but you want to be in the best state of health and frame of mind to deal with whatever may arise – and this won't be the case if you allow excess stress to take its toll.

Secondly, if you are not confronting a major problem in

your life but find yourself surrounded by any number of minor irritations, each of which adds to the burden you feel, you are less likely to deal rationally with any of them if you allow yourself to suffer physically, mentally or emotionally from the excess stress they induce.

Recognize the cause of your stressors

Excess stress can be caused by many different situations – and they are not always those which are obviously bad. Think of the situation in any home where a wedding is soon to take place and watch the stress building up as the great day approaches. Ask any mother how she feels just before a holiday when she has to organize the washing, the packing, the lists, the pets – not to mention her job! And what about Christmas – is it always the joyous time depicted on the cards which fall on the mat? What about all the work, and the hours – if not days – you have to spend in the company of people you may have invited as a duty rather than a pleasure? Is it any coincidence, I wonder, that statistics show that more relationships break up immediately after the Christmas period than at any other time of the year.

My particular stressor is moving house. Even when, as recently, I found the place I have always wanted and I was delighted to be going there, I could feel the stress mounting day by day in the run-up to the move – and it took some time for it to subside once I was in my new home.

And something that causes one person stress might not necessarily awaken the same reaction in someone else. It will depend greatly on their attitude to life in general, their background and what has happened to them in the past – as the following example illustrates.

Emma and Hilary were both young women working their way up the ladder in their respective careers. This process necessitated each of them taking exams at regular intervals. In theory neither of them should have had a problem as each was a hard worker, good at her job and eager to succeed. But while Emma always coped well (after the initial apprehension which most people feel when turning over an exam paper), Hilary would go to pieces and waste valuable time staring at the paper and feeling so stressed that she could not even make sense of the questions.

Why was there such a difference in their reactions? The answer lay in their past and in what had happened at the time of earlier examinations in their lives.

Emma had always been encouraged by her parents and their attitude had always been positive and supportive. Most parents want their child to perform as well as possible but the sensible ones realize that putting pressure on that child is not the way to achieve this result. So, when the first school exams approached, Emma's father and mother talked to their daughter reassuring her that, provided she worked hard and did the best she could, they would be perfectly satisfied, whatever the result.

Because she did not feel unduly pressurized, Emma was able to study without being overtaken by anxiety. When the day of the exam arrived, her parents ensured that the morning began just the same as any other and sent her off to school with a simple 'Good luck' and a kiss and hug as usual.

Hilary's life was not quite the same. Extremely bright and a hard worker, she began to feel the strain of her parents' expectations as soon as revision time came around. 'Are you studying hard?', 'You know how important these exams are', 'You don't want to fail, do you?' were the phrases that rang in her ears as she tried to study. The more anxious she became, the more hours she spent at her books – but the less she seemed able to absorb. She began to sleep fitfully, feeling more tired when she woke than when she went to bed.

When the day of an exam arrived, Hilary's mother would remind her 'not to let us down'. By the time she turned over the paper, Hilary could feel her heart racing, her mouth was dry, her hands were shaking and her brain appeared to have ceased functioning – all typical symptoms, of course, of excess stress. When the exam was over, the poor girl would feel so ill that she would usually go home and go straight to bed, only to lie there and worry about all the mistakes she might have made.

Because she was a hard worker and because she was naturally bright, Hilary still managed to pass her exams at school and obtain her degree at university – although she never did herself full justice, her marks not reflecting her true ability. But the wear and tear on her physical and mental strength was very great.

What is important?

The things that cause us stress vary according to age, circumstances and events which have already occurred in our lives. To the young teenager, not having the same designer-label trainers as everybody else can seem a tragedy, and most people know the desolation felt when the 'love of your life' turns out not to be interested or when that dream house is snapped up by someone else.

Go back to any of those people after a period of time has elapsed and you will find that the teenager has forgotten the trainers, another love has come along to take the place of the first and the house you finally found is far better than the one you originally wanted. But this does not mean that the stress at the time was not real.

Anyone who has suffered a tragedy in life will tend to look at things with a different eye afterwards. For them, all those minor irritations which used to be so stressful now cease to have any relevance at all.

The son of one of my patients survived a near fatal road accident, making a full recovery in spite of the doctors' gloomy predictions. No longer does his mother lose her temper when she finds dirty football boots in the kitchen – they are proof that she still has her son.

Another woman, who went through a near-death experience after a serious operation, told me that her whole attitude to life had drastically altered. Where once she had put up with an irascible boss because she was so frightened of losing her job, had been a 'doormat' (her term) to a bullying husband and was too nervous to complain about shoddy goods or poor service, she had now changed.

Feeling that, because her life had almost ended, she was being given another chance, this woman decided that life had to be lived as fully as possible and that there was no time to be anything other than assertive if that life was to be a fruitful and positive one. She had been through such a traumatic experience that she could no longer be bothered to worry about all those hitherto stressful situations.

In the course of a single week both Stella and Eve were involved in car accidents. Fortunately no one was injured in either case – the only damage suffered was to the cars and the tempers of those concerned.

Stella is the daughter of an international commodities dealer and the wife of a successful businessman. She has a part-time job with a market research organization which she enjoys, although she does not earn a great deal (and indeed treats what she does earn as pin money). The accident caused her a great deal of stress – not only at the time but for weeks afterwards. She fretted about it and talked about it incessantly to anyone who would listen, even though the damage was only superficial and the costs of repair were being met fully by the insurance company.

Like Stella, Eve had no real money worries, but six months before the accident her husband had died from cancer. Of course she was upset to have been involved in an accident – particularly one for which she was not to blame – but once the initial reaction had died down she was able to tell herself that no one had been hurt and the damage to her car had been comparatively slight – and put the whole thing out of her mind. Eve did not suffer any long-term stress because, compared to what she had gone through during the last months of her husband's life, the matter was a trivial one.

What are your personal stressors? I wonder whether you know. Stop now and think. Do you agonize over the future or are you prepared to wait and see what happens? Does an untidy house make you want to scream – or do you even notice it? Does your job drive you mad – or can you put it all behind you as soon as you leave for home?

Make a list now of all those things which cause you excess stress – and don't waste time worrying whether you are foolish to react to them. For the moment we are concerned not with whether or not you *should* be stressed by such situations but with the fact that you *are*.

Once you have your list, rate each item on a scale of 1 to 5 – petty annoyances rating 1 while situations which make you want to tear your hair and scream rate 5.

The reason for making this list is that if you are to deal effectively with those things which cause you stress, you need to understand and be aware of just what they are. If you recognize the effect a certain situation has on you, perhaps you will be able to take avoiding action beforehand so that the effect is lessened. At the very least, you should be able to acknowledge to yourself afterwards that the situation is one of your major stressors and do something to overcome any possible harmful effects it may have had.

Stress and your health

It is now widely accepted that excess stress is the cause of many health problems, some of which can be fatal. In his book *Overcoming Stress*, Dr Vernon Coleman states: 'The effects of stress on the body are so far-reaching that no organs remain unaffected and there are few diseases which are not made worse by stress. Tension and anxiety produce physiological changes in the body and those changes are in the long run often harmful.'

The health problems caused range from headaches to heart attacks, from indigestion to cancer. No one is saying that these and other problems arise only because of stress, but it is certainly a major contributory factor.

Dr Donald Meichenbaum in *Coping with Stress* writes: 'At worst, exposure to a number of stressful life events may serve to increase one's overall susceptibility to illness, possibly because they are likely to disrupt an individual's everyday activities, whether social activities, eating and sleep habits or simply the general routine of self-care.'

And it is a fact that when people are under stress – particularly women – the first thing to deteriorate is usually the way they look after themselves. How many times have we seen a harassed mother trying to help her children find their sports clothes, prepare their sandwiches for lunch and collect their homework while at the same time getting herself ready to face the day at work? And what happens? She doesn't find time for breakfast.

And what about the woman who lives alone who is either too tired or too apathetic to do anything more than the essentials when she gets in from work in the evening? On many occasions she is too stressed to prepare a nutritious meal for herself.

None of this matters if it only occurs on isolated occasions. It is the regular failure to find time for herself and to care for herself which is going to cause problems. No time to eat properly, no time to take regular exercise, never catching up with those chores, always rushing to meet deadlines at work, so exhausted that she falls asleep in front of the television at night – and then too tired to sleep when she gets to bed, finally falling asleep in the early hours of the morning only to find that she oversleeps next day; this makes her late, so there is no time for breakfast . . . This is the sort of vicious circle which can lead to serious health problems.

It is widely accepted now that excess stress can be the cause of some types of cancer. If one looks back over a period of two to three years in an individual's life immediately prior to the evidence of cancer, it is often possible to find a series of highly stressful occurrences. This is not to say that every-one who experiences a stressful period in life is going to develop cancer; it is possible that a predisposition to the disease already exists, but since there are ways of preventing stress from doing you great harm, surely it makes sense to try and use them to avoid unpleasant situations before they arise.

As well as those health conditions which can be traced directly back to excess stress, there are many which are made many times worse when such stress arises and is not dealt with.

Conditions such as migraine, eczema, psoriasis, irritable bowel syndrome, asthma, ulcers – and many others – may have an underlying physical cause. However, any sufferer will tell you that symptoms increase and are far worse during a period of stress.

The stress of anticipation

While much excess stress may be caused by things which occur in the life of the sufferer, it is probable that even more is caused by those things which *never* happen. The clue to this lies in all those statements which begin 'What if . . .' or 'Suppose . . .'. 'What if I make a fool of myself at that interview?', 'Suppose the plane crashes', 'What if Sandy is bullied when she starts school?', 'Suppose I lose my job – how will I manage?'

Whatever the particular fear or anxiety, no one can prom-ise that it will definitely never happen. Aeroplanes do crash; children are bullied and people are made redundant. But in many cases the feared situation never actually arises. Yet the worry will already have caused a tremendous amount of excess stress – with all the possible harmful effects that entails.

If you are already worried about some possible disaster in

the future, there is no point anyone saying to you 'put it out of your mind' – you just won't be able to do so. So why not look at the situation in detail and decide, firstly, what avoiding action you can take and, secondly, what you would do should the worst happen. Once you have your plan of action prepared you are far more likely to be able to put the problem out of your mind and thereby reduce your stress.

> Annie and Jim always took a two-week holiday in the summer and they liked to go abroad where they could be sure of sunshine. As the date of the holiday approached Annie would begin to worry. 'Suppose the luggage goes astray . . . what if their flight is delayed and they have to sit around the airport for hours . . . suppose the hotel is awful . . . what if their house is burgled while they are away.'
>
> Jim, on the other hand, would think to himself: 'Only another couple of weeks and we can get away. I'm really looking forward to lazing on the beach in all that sunshine, swimming in the pool, sitting in a little café in the evenings, sipping cool drinks and watching the world go by – it will be wonderful.'
>
> However their holiday turns out, Jim will already have derived some pleasure from it, while for Annie, even if it is the holiday of her dreams, much of its benefit will have been spoiled before she even begins to pack her suitcase. What a waste!

Stress and your confidence

It is not difficult to see how damaged your confidence and your self-esteem can become when you suffer repeatedly or continuously from stress. While some people function well under pressure, many do not.

In a test or examination situation, a little bit of stress may help you to think more clearly, but an extreme amount certainly will not. Even if you have studied hard and know your subject, if you allow yourself to be taken over by stress, your mind seems to go blank and even obvious answers escape you.

When it is all over and the immediate source of the excess stress no longer exists, you remember all those things you should have known when questioned. The natural reaction then is to be cross with yourself, to think that you have made a fool of yourself by appearing to know less than you really do. Your confidence is thus further eroded.

Whether the situation involves an exam, coping well with an emergency, dealing with the pressures of your job or any other incident which puts you under great pressure, the result is the same. Feeling that you have let yourself down in some way is bound to destroy your confidence. Being less confident means that you doubt your ability to cope with other stressful situations in the future – and so the downward spiral begins.

Learn to relax

As you go through this book, you will see many different stress-inducing situations and, I hope, learn how to deal with them so that they do not cause you any harm. But what about now? Suppose you are already feeling stressed – what can you do?

The one thing it is essential to learn is how to relax properly. Although this is something everyone can learn, it is not always as easy as you might think. Too many people equate relaxation with not being busy. 'I relax in front of the television at night,' they say. Or, 'I relax by having a couple of drinks.'

There is nothing at all wrong with sitting and watching television or having a drink or two if you want to. But if your body is still tense and your mind racing, that is not relaxation.

The relaxation technique given here is a very basic one and it need take no more than ten minutes of your busy day. You have seen what stress can do so surely it is worth giving up ten minutes a day in order to improve – and possibly even save – your life.

This sort of relaxation is not going to change any of the things around you which are causing you stress. You are still going to have to learn the best way of dealing with each of those. What it *will* do is prevent all those stressful things doing you any physical, mental or emotional harm in the meantime.

Basic relaxation technique

1 Do this at a time of day when you know you have no impending urgent appointment or vital task to perform. In bed at night, just before going to sleep, is ideal – but any quiet time will do. (And it is even worth getting up ten minutes earlier or going to bed ten minutes later if you truly cannot find any other time.)

2 Choose a quiet place where you will not be disturbed by other people or the telephone. Make sure that it is warm enough to enable you to relax.

3 Make yourself comfortable. Some people prefer to lie down while others like to sit up. It really doesn't matter which you choose – but do make sure that your head and neck are supported if you are sitting.

4 You may like to practise this in absolute silence or you may wish to listen to gentle music (preferably without words).

5 Close your eyes and take a couple of deep breaths – breathing from your diaphragm so that your ribcage expands as you do so.

6 Remember that the more a muscle is tensed, the more it will relax when that tension is released. So, starting with the muscles in your feet, tense them, hold the tension for about five seconds and then release them.

7 Continue doing the same thing to each set of muscles all

the way up your body – legs, thighs, hands, arms, trunk of the body, chest, shoulders, neck, jaw and head. Pay particular attention to the last four as these are the areas where tension is most greatly felt.

8 Now spend some minutes concentrating on your breathing as you breathe deeply and rhythmically from your diaphragm.

9 Remain like this for as long as you wish – but ideally it should be at least ten minutes if you are to feel the benefit.

(You may find that the first few times you practise this relaxation – particularly if it is new to you – unwanted thoughts come into your mind about all those things which are worrying you or the number of jobs you have to do tomorrow. This is perfectly normal. What you must not do is get angry with them for intruding or try to *force* them out of your mind. Simply acknowledge them and mentally put them aside for the next ten minutes, to be picked up again when you have finished your relaxation period.)

Anyone can learn to relax – though it takes practice to do it well. You can do it. Starting now, you can help yourself to feel better.

Chapter Two

Making Decisions

Making decisions, at any stage of life, can be extremely stressful. Few of us are fortunate enough to know precisely what we want, what is best for us and what is best for anyone else concerned. Indeed, there is hardly ever a solution which is as cut and dried as that. Most of the decisions we make involve a certain amount of compromise – if not crossed fingers and hoping for the best.

So when there is a decision to be made – particularly if it is one which we consider very important – there is usually a great deal of agonizing beforehand, followed by a certain amount of doubt afterwards. 'Did I do the right thing?', 'What if I've made a terrible mistake?', 'What will other people think of me?'

Other people – even those who mean well and have only our best interests at heart – often make decisions even more difficult for us. They can only see things from their own viewpoint and think how they would act in a similar situation. But what is right for someone else is not necessarily right for you. So by all means listen to the views of well-intentioned and caring people but remember that, in the end, the only person to make a decision for you can be *you*.

Considering others

It is rare for any important decision to concern one person only, so when making up your mind you may well find that you are taking other people into account and considering what would be best for them as well as for you. This is fine provided it is only part of the process and provided you don't allow yourself to become a 'doormat decision maker' who puts everyone else first and yourself right at the bottom of the list of people to be considered.

When it came to decision making, Fiona always set out to please everyone else without considering herself at all – and it didn't matter whether the decisions were to do with really important matters concerning the family or whether it was a case of what to make for supper.

If the children wanted to watch a particular programme on television just when the next instalment of her favourite serial was on the other channel, she always did what they wanted. When it came to family outings and holidays, she would always choose places she thought would appeal to her husband and sons without ever mentioning what *she* would have liked to do.

Just think what Fiona was saying about herself. She was indicating that she had such a low opinion of her own worth that her views were not worth considering at all.

She was, in fact, silently teaching her family to become even more selfish. If you act as if you were unimportant, that is how others will come to treat you. And, since her children were sons, think what sort of impression she was unintentionally giving them of how women deserve to be regarded.

Everyone with a family knows that there has to be a certain amount of give and take and that sometimes we cook a meal, take part in an activity or journey to a place which would not be our first choice. That is part of the natural compromise process whenever a number of people are involved. But if we are prepared to make compromises, others should be too – and it is certainly something we should be teaching our children.

I'm not talking about the kind of compromise which would involve doing something against one's principles, simply about kindness and consideration. If one member of the family is prepared to stand in the cold and rain to cheer on another who is taking part in a football match when really they would far rather be sitting at home with a good book, then it should not be too much to expect that football player to show the same consideration by joining in some activity which might not be his or her ideal way of passing the time.

The media does not always help. While there are some programmes or articles which do their best to be fair and to consider all sides of a question, there are certainly others which are aggressively militant in the statement of their opinions – particularly where women are concerned. Whether in public or private life, everyone is entitled to his or her opinion but no one is entitled to force that opinion on someone else.

Peer pressure and self-esteem

The stress of decision making can start at a very young age. Many young people are led into patterns of behaviour which do not naturally appeal to them because they are frightened of being 'different' or left out by their friends and acquaintances.

Peer pressure can influence decisions at all levels – from choosing to wear certain clothes or hairstyles, through petty shoplifting in order to be accepted as part of a seemingly desirable gang, to indulging in under-age sex because 'everyone does it'.

When a young girl feels unhappy about how she is acting but feels that she is caught in a trap and has no choice but to go on in the same way, she begins to dislike herself. This can show itself in many ways – from complete withdrawal to highly aggressive behaviour. But one of the more serious consequences of self-hate – however it is caused – is the onset of potentially life-threatening eating disorders.

One of the greatest gifts we can give our child – boy or girl – is that of self-esteem. He or she needs to know that they are a valued individual in their own right and that although their opinion is not the only one to be taken into consideration, it certainly counts. Someone with well-developed self-esteem will be able to act in the way which they consider best for themselves – without ever having to be confrontational about doing so.

A child's self-esteem, however, is a fragile thing and needs constant nurturing. It can easily be shattered, particularly when there is conflict between the parents. Many children faced with the break-up of their family because of separation or divorce feel either that they are in some way to blame for the situation or that one or both of the adults concerned will no longer love them. At times like this it is important to reassure children constantly that neither of those cases is true and that, whatever happens between the adults, they will always be loved and appreciated by both parents.

There are also times when you might not realize how children are feeling. It is so easy, for example, for them to be excluded at a time of great anxiety in the family. This may be done with the best intentions in the world, but children are extremely sensitive to the atmosphere around them and if no explanation is given when that atmosphere is tense or negative, they will usually assume the worst.

Sally was only ten when her maternal grandfather had a stroke which left him severely handicapped and unable to speak. She was never told what had happened but was astute enough to be aware that something was very wrong. Jane, her mother, was obviously distressed by her father's condition and anxious about his future, but thinking she was doing the best for her daughter, did what she could to hide her true feelings in front of the child. When, just a few weeks later, the old man died, Jane still did not say anything to Sally.

Think of it from the child's point of view. One moment everything at home was the same as it had always been. The next day all was changed. Although she never saw her mother cry, Sally was obviously aware that she was not her usual self – and sometimes she heard quiet sobs and low voices coming from her parents' bedroom. Then the house was full of people with dark clothes, sad eyes and long faces. On top of all this, she was no longer taken on a Sunday afternoon to visit Grandma and Grandpa, something she had always loved.

The only conclusion Sally's young mind could come to was that she must have done something very wrong to be punished like this – no fun in the house . . . everyone quiet and serious . . . no sitting on Grandpa's lap after tea on a Sunday afternoon while he asked her silly riddles. What a punishment! And the longer the situation continued, the more she felt that she must be a really bad person.

It was several weeks before Jane felt up to telling her daughter what had really happened, but by then the damage had been done. Although Sally's logical mind accepted the truth of what had happened, her self-esteem did not fully recover for a long time afterwards.

What Jane had done had been with her daughter's best interests at heart. She did not want to distress her and she felt that as she might break down when talking about her father, the child would be adversely affected by her own grief. But what we imagine is often so much more dreadful than what happens in reality – and in this case Jane did, in fact, make matters worse.

Multiple choices

As they pass through their teenage years, girls and young women are faced with a number of decisions, many of which will greatly affect their long-term future. Here, too, their opinion of their own self-worth will influence the choices they make.

For both girls and boys there are, of course, important decisions to be made about future careers and the type of education needed to move in the appropriate direction. Such considerations must have been so much easier for women before the Second World War when the majority of them had no choice to make. Unless they had a true vocation and were dedicated to following a particular career path, most women settled for the fact that they would have fairly basic jobs which they would work at until such time as they married. There were no anxieties about deciding whether to go to university and then carve out a career or stay at home and bring up a family.

I am not for a moment saying that the situation as it existed pre-1940 was an ideal one – simply that following an accepted direction rather than making a decision was a far less stressful state of affairs for the women concerned.

Whatever decision a girl makes about the future path she would prefer to follow, fate can so easily take a hand and throw even more decisions in front of her.

Joanna thought she knew just what she wanted. A bright girl who had always excelled at school, she wanted very much to go to university and then make a career for herself. She felt that she would probably want a home and family one day but that this was not likely to be until much later on.

Everything seemed to be going her way. She passed the necessary exams and gained entrance to the university of her choice. The summer before she became an undergraduate she met Mark who was five years older and working in an import agency. The young couple fell deeply in love and suddenly life did not seem so straightforward to Joanna any more. There were so many questions to be answered, so many decisions to make.

Should she continue with her studies? If so, should she go ahead with her plans to study at a university so far from home that she would see Mark only during the vacations? Should she settle for a less academic course and stay at home so that her relationship with Mark could develop? Which sacrifice would be the greater and which would she be more likely to regret in the future?

To give him his due, Mark tried hard not to influence Joanna's decision. He truly wanted the best for the girl he loved. But when they were together, the passion and intensity of their love for each other *was* an influence on her. Her parents, who were fond of Mark and were happy for Joanna to be seeing him, nevertheless did all they could to persuade her to take up her university place and follow her original plans. All Joanna's friends had an opinion on the matter too – and in the end the poor girl did not know what she wanted or how to make the best decision.

Eventually Joanna made up her mind. She decided to go ahead with her studies but to change to a university nearer home so that she would be able to see Mark from time to time during the term. But in the time which elapsed between the problem arising and the decision being made, she suffered a great deal of excess stress which affected both her eating and sleeping – and could, therefore, have adversely affected her studies.

Such choices do not affect only the very young. At any age a woman can be faced with the decision of whether to concentrate on her career or her home and marriage/partnership. Indeed the stress induced can be even greater as the woman gets older; and if she is ultimately to have children, the time left for doing so grows ever shorter.

Just think of some of the decisions which need to be made by a woman in that position today. Should she continue her career path or choose early marriage and children – or try and combine both? Should she marry her partner or live with him? Here too the choice she makes may well be affected by the views of other people – not only the man himself but her parents and friends. Unless she is very strong it is extremely difficult not to be swayed in all directions by the views of these other – usually well-intentioned – people.

And once she is married or living with a partner, does she want children? This is another decision which has grown more difficult over the years. Although there were always some exceptions to the rule, it was generally the case in our mothers' and grandmothers' time that a married woman would go on to have children unless this proved to be impossible. There was rarely a choice to be made.

There was no contraceptive pill – and methods of birth control, even if used, tended to be less reliable than they are today. So there was far less choice about when to have babies. On the other hand, if they did not come along naturally, there was often little to be done about the situation. Hormone treatment, IVF, surrogate mothers and the like were not options for the women of yesterday. Abortions were illegal and sterilization was undertaken only when the woman's medical condition made it essential.

Of course we should be grateful for medical progress and for changes in social attitude – no longer are young women sent to psychiatric institutions simply because they have given birth to illegitimate children – but with progress comes choice. And with choice comes the stress which accompanies having to make difficult decisions.

> One of my patients who had great difficulty in conceiving because of her husband's low sperm count opted for IVF treatment. Not only was this very expensive – and they were not rich people – but it was not guaranteed to be successful. So there was stress during the waiting time to see if it had, in fact, worked. Then there was the stress of discovering that it had not . . . and the stress of trying to save for another attempt while aware that the biological clock was constantly ticking away. Then the stress of waiting for the results of the second treatment. I am happy to say that the second treatment resulted in the birth of a delightful baby girl, much adored by her doting parents. But both husband and wife suffered greatly from symptoms of excess stress during all that time.

Aiming for perfection

A lot of women today find themselves performing the juggling act of coping with home, family and job – and trying to do each to the best of their ability. We've all seen the television commercials. There's the one where the elegantly groomed woman – all shoulder pads and scarlet fingernails – comes home to her spotless house and happy family. Preferring the casual look for evening, she zips up her designer jeans with one hand while changing her hairstyle from chignon to pony tail with the other (and all without chipping the polish on those nails!). She puts plates of nutritious fun food in front of her well-behaved children while at the same time preparing a delightful meal for herself, her husband and the four beautiful friends who are later to be found sitting round the roaring log fire in the sitting room (presumably while some good fairy does the washing up).

Is that what your life is like? No, nor is mine. Even so, why should such bits of nonsense as a television commercial cause us any stress when we all know it doesn't portray a true picture? There are two reasons for this. Firstly, anything that is repeated often enough will have an effect on the person who hears/sees it. That is the premise on which all advertising is based. If it didn't work, companies would not be so eager to spend hundreds of thousands of pounds on promoting their products year after year.

> A friend of mine was married for several years to a man who delighted in telling her how stupid she was. She was an intelligent woman who held down a good job and knew that she was not stupid. But by the time that marriage came to an end she had heard the words so often that her confidence had been eroded and it took some time for her to regain it.

Secondly, most women today who are home-makers had mothers, grandmothers or aunts who never worked outside the home and so had plenty of time to plump up cushions, starch linen and arrange fresh flowers in every room. We know that if we have a full-time job there is no way that we will have the time or the energy to keep everything to those same demanding standards. And yet we try. We want to be perfect home-makers, perfect mothers and perfect at our jobs.

No wonder there is stress. There is stress if we try to do everything and either fail or become so exhausted that we are not fit company for the rest of the family. There is the stress caused by our own guilt if we don't even make the effort.

There are only so many waking hours in the day. And as you will see when we come to deal with how to cope with stress, some of that time should be reserved just for you. (No, don't laugh and throw the book away. I promise I'll show you how you can achieve this miracle.)

Take a look at your priorities. List those tasks – at home and/or at work – that *must* be done. Then list those that are not essential but which you enjoy doing. (Some people love to cook and find it relaxing, while others believe that life is too short to stuff a mushroom.) Finally, make a list of tasks which can be handed out to other members of the family or – if the budget runs to it – you can pay someone else to do. And forget anything which doesn't find its way on to one of those lists. Life still goes on if there is a layer of dust on the mantelpiece; the world will not come to an end just because you use frozen pastry instead of making your own from scratch. Do what you can and don't feel guilty about the rest.

(I know that I am ignoring the existence of 'new man' here – I am certain he exists somewhere and that there are couples who really share everything from filling in the crossword to emptying the rubbish bin – but I'm afraid that in the majority of cases household tasks are still done primarily by the woman, whether or not she has a job outside the home.)

Guilt

Guilt – over things done or not done, said or not said – is one of the greatest causes of excess stress. And since the perfect person does not exist (and what a bore she would be if she did), each of us is at some time going to have cause to feel guilty.

Apart from being the source of a great deal of stress, guilt is a waste of energy and emotion. It can also cause real physical harm. In his book *Mind Over Body*, Dr Vernon Coleman writes: 'Guilt is a major cause of heart disease, stomach ulceration, asthma, skin conditions and a hundred and one other problems.'

Are you someone who is in the habit of feeling guilty? If so, try asking yourself whether you are really as bad as you instinctively think or whether your opinion of yourself has been coloured by the view of one or more of the people around you.

Quite often you will find that someone in your life – particularly someone who was around as you were growing up – has instilled in you the thought that everything is always your fault. Whether this was done in anger or by quiet manipulation, such behaviour is a form of aggression – and aggressive attitudes are displayed by those who have a low self-image and can only make themselves feel big or important by belittling someone else.

So before you allow yourself to suffer from feelings of guilt, take some time to work out whether there is a reason for these feelings to be there in the first place. And if there is no reason, what can you do about it?

In an ideal world you would distance yourself from the person whose words or behaviour are causing you to feel guilty. But this is not an ideal world and such action is not always possible – sometimes the person is a close member of the family or even your boss.

If contact is inevitable, try to see that person as someone to be pitied rather than feared. If they are so insecure that they need to act aggressively, they are poor creatures really and certainly inferior in character to those they attempt to intimidate. In many cases this alteration in the way you think of them is enough to take the sting out of their words so that they are never again able to make you feel guilty.

But suppose your feelings of guilt have arisen because you really have done something which you consider to be wrong – what then?

First you have to be honest with yourself and consider whether what you did was deliberate or accidental. If accidental, then do forgive yourself because there is not one of us who has not done something wrong by accident. This doesn't mean that you shouldn't do whatever you can to put the situation right – and ensure that it doesn't happen again, of course.

Perhaps what you did was deliberate – and such words or actions can take many forms. One person may temporarily be spiteful while another may be criminally dishonest. One may be malicious, another deceitful.

Whatever has caused you to feel guilty, the stages in dealing with it are the same.

1 If what you did caused upset or hurt to someone else – whether this was deliberate or not – you need to apologize.
2 If there is some way in which you can put matters right, do so. If you damaged an item, perhaps you can replace it. If it was someone else's feelings which were damaged, you will need to prove by your words and your actions that you are doing your best to make amends.
3 If there is nothing you can do to put things right, all you can do is resolve to ensure that the same thing can never happen again – and then put the matter out of your mind. All the self-torture in the world cannot change the past but it can certainly affect you and your present and future wellbeing.
4 Learn from the situation. Whether you have been able to make amends or not, if you have learned from your mistake the experience will not have been wholly

negative. If you believe that we are on a spiritual path where important lessons need to be learned – or just want a happier and less stressful life – knowledge of yourself and your potential weaknesses (as well as how you intend to overcome them) can be highly valuable.

5 Finally, put the guilt-making incident behind you. Thinking further about it serves no purpose at all and will simply contribute to making you a negative person who is susceptible to excess stress.

When she was 17, Andrea had stolen some money from the till in the shop where she worked. It had not been an enormous amount and no one had ever discovered what she had done. But the feelings of guilt remained with Andrea for years and, even though she never did anything like it again, she developed a very low opinion of herself which affected the whole of her life. She went into relationships with the most unsuitable men – most of whom treated her badly (which was what she felt she deserved) – and she only put herself forward for jobs which were well beneath her capabilities.

When Andrea came to see me it was for help in improving her self-confidence and, during the course of the first consultation, she told me what she had done all those years ago. I suggested she worked through the steps already mentioned. This is how the numbered steps related to Andrea's situation.

1 There was no doubt that she had stolen the cash deliberately. She had not planned it in advance but had taken advantage of an opportunity which arose, knowing all the while precisely what she was doing. Because the shop in which she had worked no longer existed and she did not know what had happened to the owner, Andrea was not able to apologize to anyone.

2 It was obviously difficult for her to put matters right in that she did not know anyone to whom she could return the money. Yet she still felt a great need to do so.

3 Although she had been adamant that she would never do such a thing again, she had been plagued by guilt ever since. As she could not return the money to its

rightful owner I asked her whether she thought there was anything else she could do. She suggested that she might give a sum to charity. Because the sum needed to be big enough for her to feel that she had made reparation, Andrea donated an entire week's wages. This meant that she had to struggle financially and do without many of the things she normally took for granted, but she felt that this was part of the 'putting right' process.

4 What had Andrea learned from the situation? She had certainly found that the temporary elation at having enough extra cash to buy one or two luxury items was not worth the agony of waiting to see whether she would be found out and then, when she was not, suffering the pangs of guilt and self-hate which had beset her ever since.

5 Could she now forgive herself? Andrea and I discussed whether any positive purpose would be served by her continuing dislike of herself and guilt about what she had done. Realizing how her guilt was crippling her life and also causing her to suffer the physical symptoms of stress, Andrea felt that she would now be able to let go of the guilt and face the future more positively.

Check-list for decision making

We have seen how stressful it can be when important decisions have to be made about our lives. Now let's look at the best way of going about making those decisions.

1 Do it sooner rather than later. I am not advocating snap decisions with no consideration at all, but the longer you put off sitting down and working out what you are going to do, the more likely you are to suffer the effects of excess stress. Remember that anticipation is often the greatest cause of stress because much anticipation happens to be negative.

2 By all means listen to other people's opinions – particularly if you know that those people care about you and

have your best interests at heart. But do remember that no two people begin at the same starting point; we are all coloured by what has happened to *us* in the past and can give opinions based only on our own experiences. So bear in mind ultimately that the decisions must be yours.

3 What would you do if there was no one to consider but yourself? What do you really want and what does your intuition tell you is right for you? You may never be able to do exactly this – we all have other people in our lives who have to be considered – but at least you will have been honest with yourself about your true desires.

4 Work out your options, bearing in mind the other people who really do need to be considered. Remember that these are the people who are going to be affected in some way – not those whose feelings might be a little bruised because you did not take their advice.

5 If you do make a wrong decision, what is the worst that could happen? In your imagination, follow through each possible scenario, thinking how the future might turn out. Consider what would be the greatest disaster if you went down the wrong road – and decide what you would do in such a case. There are very few situations which could not be satisfactorily handled, although there may be a period of shaky finances or a feeling of having been foolish to contend with. Ask yourself whether you could cope with that worst possible outcome and work out how you would do so.

6 Now that you know you could cope with the worst, anything else must be better. So there should now be nothing to prevent you making your decision.

7 As soon as possible after making your decision, act upon it. The more you allow yourself to brood, the greater the doubt which will form in your mind – and you will find yourself having to begin the whole decision-making process all over again.

No one claims that making decisions is easy – it rarely is, mainly because there are very few people who have no one but themselves to consider (and they would often prefer the situation to be otherwise). But the stress caused by not making those decisions, or by not acting upon the decisions you make, is far more devastating than any problems which might result from the decisions themselves.

Chapter Three

The Working Woman

While some women choose to stay at home with their children while they are small, the majority today do work outside the home – some because they really want to, some because financial considerations make it imperative, and most for a combination of the two reasons.

There are so many different types of women holding down a vast diversity of jobs that, for the most part, it is impossible to generalize about the problems they encounter. One thing does appear to be common to the vast majority, however, and that is the level of excess stress they tend to suffer. The difficult situations faced by the high-flying, globe-trotting career woman may be completely different to those confronting the woman on the check-out till at the supermarket, but the resulting stress with its incumbent symptoms is often very similar.

Organizing your life

No one wants to live a life so organized and strictly time-tabled that all the fun and spontaneity goes out of it, but juggling home and work does entail a certain amount of organization. Not only do you have to plan for all those times when things are going well but you have also to be prepared for the crises which can occur in any life.

These crises can arise whether you live alone or with a husband or partner – and particularly if you have children. The single woman has to cope with all the responsibilities of her job, her home and her finances. She also has to find someone to be there if the plumber is due to call or tiles have blown off in a gale. Of course, if you have sufficient money, you can pay someone else to do this for you but the ultimate responsibility is yours and it is just one more thing to add to your already mounting pile of pressures.

And what about those days when you have an accident or just wake up feeling ill? If the situation is really serious, matters will be taken out of your hands by doctors or hospitals; but suppose it is just a dose of flu? Although you feel dreadful and just want to stay in bed and have warm drinks, it will be you who has to get up and make them – there is no one else around to supply warm drinks or sympathy. And who is going to feed the cat or take the dog for a walk, to make sure there is some food in the house, to go out and collect a prescription from the chemist? Yes, with the help of good friends or neighbours, all these problems can be solved, but even thinking about them adds to the tension already surrounding you.

And that's before you start wondering about what is happening at work. If you are away for too long, will you lose some money this month? If you normally deal with correspondence, how will you ever cope with the mountain of paperwork which is going to be waiting for you on your return? Did you remember to cancel those appointments? What will happen if you are not at the meeting to give your point of view?

If you are self-employed, matters are often even more stressful. While there are insurance policies to cover your income should you have a serious accident or illness or need a stay in hospital, no one is going to compensate you for a blinding headache, a streaming cold or a dose of flu – all things which could reduce or even destroy your earning power until you feel better.

The crises that the working mother encounters may be different but can be just as stressful. While most employers will be understanding if your child has an accident or becomes suddenly ill, what happens when there is a more long-term problem? This does not even have to be something life-threatening or dramatic; a simple dose of chicken-pox is enough to necessitate a child being at home for a prolonged period. The mother then needs to decide whether to take the entire time off work to be with the child who needs her, or to enlist the help of a friend and relative and get back to work as soon as possible. There is no right solution; you can only do whatever you feel is best. But whichever decision you make, your stress level is likely to increase. If you stay at home you may worry about whether you will have a job to go back to; if you return to work, you will probably feel guilty about 'deserting' your sick child – even if he or she is being looked after by a loving grandmother.

When you are organizing your life so that work, home and social activities are all being catered for, think about the possible crises too. We all hope that they will never happen but your stress level is likely to be far lower if you are prepared for the problems before they arise.

Dealing with a crisis

1   Take a moment to stop and think. Take a few deep breaths to dispel the worst of the stress and help you collect your thoughts. Even if the situation is grave enough to necessitate calling the emergency services, you are likely to be clearer in your head and do this more efficiently if you do stop and think than if you do it in a panic,

2   What is the problem? What are your objectives and what do you need to achieve?

3 Prioritize. What must be done first? Think about people you need to notify, arrangements you may need to make.
4 Once the immediate situation is under control, take the time to think about what needs to be done in the immediate and even the long-term future. Make a list of all that must be achieved and work your way through that list.
5 Communicate. Who else needs to know of the situation which has arisen? Perhaps your employer so that arrangements can be made to cover your absence; perhaps your child's school needs to be informed; you may need to contact a friend or relative if you yourself need help.
6 When the crisis situation is over, sit down and evaluate the situation and the resources you had to cope with it. Could things have been managed better? Is there anything you would do differently another time?

How to prepare for a possible future crisis

You will already have spent time organizing the running of your home and work life so that the wheels turn as smoothly as possible. Now you should try and list all the possible crises someone in your position might encounter and see if you could make a contingency plan for each.

For example, if you work in an office, you could make sure that someone else there knows where you keep specific files in case you are forced to be absent one day. Perhaps that same person could be kept up to date with particular situations so that he or she would be able to deputize for you at comparatively short notice.

If you have young children, you might be able to come to some reciprocal arrangement with another mother so that either of you would be prepared to help out with the other's family should the need arise.

Every situation is different so only you can work out

contingency plans for your particular lifestyle. Having such plans in reserve – hopefully never to be needed – can eradicate at least part of the excess stress facing any working woman.

Cooperation

If you do not live alone, you will have to obtain the cooperation of other members of the household. You are not superwoman and even if you feel that you could cope with everything every single day, it is not a good idea to do so. What sort of message would you be sending to the other members of the family? You would be telling them that either you consider them useless and so have to take all the burdens on your own shoulders or you are someone not worthy of consideration at all.

Just as the efficient businesswoman has to learn to delegate, so too must any woman trying to juggle both home and work without letting either drop. And only you can decide which tasks you are able to delegate. Obviously there will be several things to bear in mind, such as the age and abilities of other members of the family and their particular routines and timetables. Remember, however, that even quite young children can be given simple tasks to do around the home – and they will probably enjoy the responsibility. And certainly husbands or partners should be willing to take their part in the running of the household.

Making time for yourself

While you are busy making all these wonderful plans for the efficient running of your life, please make sure that you build in some time just for you. Many women are very bad at doing this and even feel guilty if they sit and watch television unless they are doing some knitting or stuffing envelopes at the same time.

It is up to you when you take this time and how you spend it. Some people like to have half an hour a day to themselves while others prefer to take one morning a week. Some want to do something energetic like working out at a gym or digging the garden, while others prefer to sit in a deckchair or listen to music. It doesn't matter what you do as long as it is done because you *want* to and not because you *have* to.

Returning to work

Women who are returning to work after a lengthy absence – perhaps because they have remained at home to care for their children or because they were made redundant and have had difficulty in finding another job – tend to suffer greatly from stress when it comes to seeking to join the ranks of the employed again.

This stress often has the effect of greatly reducing their self-confidence so that in many cases they actually apply for jobs which are far below their capabilities. And this, of course, often means that they earn far less than they should.

One woman told me that after being employed as a secretary for many years, she had spent the last ten years at home bringing up her young family. This had been her choice and she did not regret it in the least but she was frightened when she realized how much the office world had changed since she was last part of it. Where once there had been shorthand notebooks and typewriters, now there were computers, fax machines, modems and the Internet. She did not think she would ever be able to master all these and so had settled for a lesser job where she would not be required to tackle them.

And yet there are many excellent training courses for

women returners, both in practical skills and in ways of boosting confidence and gaining assertiveness. It is worth approaching your local Training and Enterprise Council and seeking the advice of your local reference library, which will usually have details of courses specific to your own area.

Don't sell yourself short. If you have been at home caring for a family, you have at the same time been acquiring many of the skills so sought after today – time management, supervisory and communication skills, and a whole host of interpersonal techniques which will serve you well in any business.

Feeling guilty

On the whole, women are pretty good at feeling guilty about things – and this often becomes more obvious in the working woman, particularly if she has a home and family too. Let's look at some of the things which might cause these feelings of guilt.

Perhaps she fears that, because of the time spent at work, she is 'neglecting' her home. Well, maybe a few corners have to be cut when it comes to housekeeping, but is there great fulfilment in having the best polished doorstep in the street? Did anyone ever have inscribed on their tombstone, 'Beloved wife and mother – best vacuumed carpets in town'?

Now I'm not advocating living a life of squalor in a cobweb-infested house; I just feel that it is important to get one's priorities right. Of course there are certain things which have to be done, but don't forget that if you are not the only person to live there, others have to play their parts too.

You will also find your own way of cutting corners. Even if you are someone who does not like to buy ready-made meals, you might decide to start buying washed potatoes or prepared salads. If you love to cook and prepare food, then choose another way of saving time, but if it is just a chore to you, remember that such things as freshly-squeezed orange juice and ready-prepared salad dressings are available in every supermarket and can save you time on an almost daily basis.

Some women who return to work feel guilty because they are unable to spend as much time as previously with their husband or partner. This could be because their hours do not precisely coincide or because there are still many chores to be done on coming home from work.

This is where all that cooperation is so important. Could some of those chores be shared so that you are able to chat over the washing up or the weeding? Perhaps each of you could do some of them while the other one is still working? Every family will have to work out its own plan.

One couple I know agreed that as soon as both had returned from work, they would stop whatever they were doing and sit down together over a drink (sometimes tea, sometimes something stronger) and talk to each other. In summer they would sit in the garden, in winter it was in front of the fire. But whatever the time and whatever the location, it gave them both a chance to unwind from the pressures of the day and to discuss either important matters or trivia, as the fancy took them.

Val and Tom had both been out of work for a while, having been made redundant from their respective jobs. Eventually, Val managed to find another job, but, although he applied for many, Tom was not successful. Val told me how guilty she felt as she left for work each morning and came home each evening. She imagined Tom's feelings of resentment, although he never showed them to her, and also how he must feel uncomfortable because she was now the earner in the family while he had only his unemployment benefit coming in. She also imagined how he must feel about having taken over the major part of running the house – something they had done together in the past.

Strangely enough, Val never thought to *ask* Tom how he felt – she just imagined how it must be. In fact, Tom was delighted that his wife had found a job and was convinced that he too would find one soon. He felt no resentment about doing most of the housework but was pleased to help Val in this way and felt it would allow them to spend time together when she came home in the evenings.

Many problems arise in life because of lack of communication between people, especially when they are imagining what someone else is thinking. So if you have any sense of guilt because of what you *think* your partner is feeling, try sitting down together and talking and you might even find those feelings do not exist at all.

Perhaps the greatest feelings of guilt experienced by the working mother are those concerned with her children. And this often applies across the board – from the woman rich enough to afford a nanny to the one who has to rely on the kindness of a neighbour.

Rachel had no choice – she had to work. The single mother of a baby son, she had a goood job and was able to earn a reasonable salary, much of which she spent on an excellent child-minder for young Matthew.

She knew that Matthew was happy and well cared for during the day and that she could provide better for the two of them by continuing to work. And she spent as much time with her baby as possible in the evenings and at weekends. What caused her to feel both sad and guilty was that the child-minder was the one who was there on the day Matthew's first baby tooth peeped through and it was the child-minder who later saw him take his first faltering steps.

All any mother can do is decide what is best both for her and her child. Having made that decision, there will be certain arrangements – even compromises – to be made. Making compromises does not make you a bad person provided they are made in the best interests of everyone concerned.

What does matter is that, having chosen to bring your children into the world, you spend as much quality time

with them as possible. An hour playing with them and –
most important – listening to them is worth more than a
whole day trying to get them out from under your feet or
sitting them in front of the television or video. And once
they have reached school age they will be out of the house
for a great part of the day anyway and will develop their
own set of friends, hobbies and pastimes. They will also be
old enough to appreciate that most mothers go out to work
these days.

In the workplace

There is still much prejudice and discrimination to be found
in some places of work – although, fortunately, the situation
appears to be improving. Many places operate a system
based on complete equality; some pay lip service to doing so.
Even among those which advocate equality, it sometimes
seems that a woman has to work harder to prove herself than
a man.

Having said that, there have been some women who have
done their working sisters a great disservice by their aggressive attitude. Aggression – in a man or woman – never wins
in the long run, although it may seem to lead to temporary
victory. Obvious aggression is a sure sign of the insecurity of
the person acting in that way; anyone who feels confident
has no need to be aggressive.

Even in the most far-sighted organizations, because
women's equality is a comparatively new concept, there are
still occasions when no one is quite certain how to act – and
such uncertainty can only cause stress in the people
concerned.

Lynda was one of a team of three men and two women working
in the British division of an international electronics company.
The team had been together for about three years when their

supervisor left and Lynda was promoted to that position. Suddenly no one was quite sure of what was expected of them.

The work itself was no problem. Each individual knew his or her job and Lynda understood fully what was expected of her in her new supervisory role. The social side caused more of a problem. The five of them had been friends as well as colleagues for a long time and would often go out together in the evening for a drink or a meal – sometimes with their respective partners. Now Lynda was not sure whether she should go or not. After all, their previous supervisor had never been invited to join them on such occasions.

Lynda felt under pressure. If she went out with her friends and former colleagues, would they feel uneasy or would management disapprove. If she did not go, perhaps they would think she was setting herself apart from them and consider her conceited for doing so. She also wondered whether they resented her increased status and earning capacity. She felt that to ask them what they thought would make her appear weak, while not to do so seemed churlish.

In the end Lynda decided to take the initiative. She asked the other four to join her for a drink after work one evening to celebrate her promotion. They all accepted and, after a few moments of awkwardness, they spent as pleasant an hour together as they had ever done.

In this particular situation, where the people concerned knew each other well, where each was good at his or her job and where there was no resentment of Lynda's new position, this was the right solution. But it would not be so in every case. Any woman put in this position has to make her own decision based on her judgement of the people involved. The important thing is to decide on a course to follow and to put it into effect as soon as possible. Undue hesitation might seem like weakness to others (and there could be those who would seek to take advantage of it) and would certainly cause extra stress to the woman herself.

Diane's position was quite different. She was the first woman to be promoted to board level in the financial institution in which she worked. This particular organization had been run by the same – now ageing – men for many years and Diane felt that her promotion was a token one, made as the company was dragged kicking and screaming into the late 20th century.

She was good at her job. She knew this and so did they. She had no problems when it came to dealing with her staff or her colleagues. She was both liked and respected. Her frustration (and the stress that comes with it) grew out of the fact that she was hardly ever given an opportunity to express her opinion at board meetings. If she did venture a thought or a comment, the other members of the board, while seeming to be polite and courteous, actually ignored her comments and acted as if she had never made them.

This is a problem faced by many women in both large and small organizations and one which can only be dealt with by those women who are assertive enough to ensure that their views are listened to as reasonably as their position deserves.

Working away from home

If your job entails travelling – and particularly if you fre-quently have to stay away from home – there are many stresses which you may encounter.

Forget for the moment all the practical arrangements which may need to be made with home and family – that is a whole separate topic. What I am referring to here is the apprehension which many women feel when travelling alone.

This is by no means an 'anti-men' book. I fully appreciate that the vast majority of men are kind, considerate and courteous to a woman travelling and staying in hotels alone. But there are a sufficient number who are not. Even if you have never encountered any problems yourself, you will have read reports in the newspapers of assaults on lone women and these may have caused you to feel extra pressure when you are travelling.

Most women who stay in hotels alone know that there is usually at least one man who – especially after several drinks – feels that he has to prove to his colleagues what a great fellow he is by trying to proposition her. Even if you can handle the situation, and even if his colleagues apologize for him and hustle him away from the scene, such behaviour can leave you feeling unsettled. This is why so many women when travelling alone will choose to make use of room service and eat in their bedrooms rather than sitting alone in an anonymous restaurant.

Because there have been such problems, at least two of the larger hotel chains now take special care of their lone female guests. One of these has 'ladies only' floors in some of their larger hotels and both chains ensure that their bedroom doors have good locks, and spyholes too. They also instruct reception staff not to mention the room number when a woman checks in and to hand her the key wrapped round with a piece of card so that no one else can see the number.

On the one hand, it is a sad reflection of our times that such precautions are necessary. On the other, it can eliminate a great deal of stress to know that they are available.

Driving

Women driving alone can sometimes find themselves in very stressful situations.

A friend of mine was returning to London from a conference in the Midlands. It was night time and she was driving steadily along the motorway, delighted that there were no traffic delays.

Suddenly she realized that there was a car with headlights blazing right on her tail. She could hear several voices shouting as the lights were flashed. She did not know what to do; if she went faster, would it appear that she was playing some sort of game with them? If she slowed down, what would they do? Heart racing, she kept steadily on until the next exit. She left the motorway, and drove for a few miles on the lesser road before joining it again later on.

Nothing happened to her and she arrived home perfectly safely. But she had suffered unnecessary stress on that journey.

Here are a few tips given by a self-defence specialist which could be of use to you if you are likely to find yourself in similar a situation.

- Keep a mobile phone with you in your car. Even if you never use it, the fact that is there and you can call for help if you are being bothered – or simply if you break down – can bring great peace of mind.
- Avoid dangly toys in the car or amusing slogans on the back window as these are taken by some to indicate that you are a 'fun' person and would be ready for some sort of motorized game.
- Cover yourself with a scarf or shawl if you are returning from an evening function late at night and are wearing a low-cut dress. If you have glittering jewellery, remove it and put it in your handbag.
- Always lock all car doors from the inside at night.
- Keep your handbag on the floor behind your seat rather than tossed on the seat beside you.

Of course, you also have to get to your car from wherever you happen to be working or staying and this can be nerve-racking too. It is all very well for expert statisticians to reassure us that the likelihood of being attacked is very slight, but we have all read or heard of cases where it has happened and the apprehension we feel can easily send our stress levels soaring.

Here it is necessary to strike a balance between *expecting* something dreadful to happen and knowing what you would do if it did.

I'm not trying to frighten you; the number of women

attacked is really very small indeed. And if you become too apprehensive, you might even invite unwelcome attention. I am quite convinced that fear can be sensed by an aggressor and that those who think of themselves as a victim frequently become one

Be prepared

We have already seen that one of the principal causes of excess stress is apprehension – fear of something which *might* occur. So, with thanks to the same self-defence expert, here are a few points to bear in mind.

- Use your common sense when parking and do your best to leave the car in an area which is well lit, below a street lamp if possible.
- Walk in an assertive manner – head held high and with long, firm strides – as this is likely to deter any aggressor.
- If someone does approach and wants your wallet, credit cards or jewellery, let them have it. Your safety is far more valuable and many will run away as soon as they have what they want. However, drop the items on the floor so that you have time to make your escape while the aggressor is picking them up.
- If you feel that you are being followed, go to the nearest house and ring the doorbell. There is little point in shouting 'Help' as this may deter the residents from opening the door. But if you yell 'Fire' as loudly as you can, they are far more likely to appear.
- While it is illegal to carry anything which might be considered an 'offensive weapon', there is no law against carrying a heavyweight glossy magazine, rolled into a cylinder. A blow to the side of an aggressor's head will stun him sufficiently for you to make your escape.

Once you have considered what could happen and prepared yourself so that you know what you would do, try and put the whole matter out of your mind – walking about in a permanent state of fear is destructive to both health and peace of mind.

There are some jobs which tend to put women more at risk than others. The disappearance of estate agent Suzy Lamplugh, who went to show a man a property which was for sale and who was never seen again, highlighted this fact. Most companies now do what they can to ensure that their women employees are not put in a potentially dangerous situation, but there is no way that every possible danger can be catered for.

As a hypnotherapist, I often spend time alone in a room with a male patient – but in all the years I have been practising, I have never had a single problem. And it does not follow that an aggressor has to be male – there are some violent women about too.

The point I am trying to make is that it is impossible to prepare for every possible eventuality – and too much fear would make us want to do nothing but stay in bed all day, having allowed the aggressors of the world to beat us into submission. All we can do is take sensible precautions and then get on with our lives. Be aware, though, that heightened apprehension can bring excess stress. You will need to do what you can to prevent that stress doing you harm – and in this book you will find various ways to help you do that.

Chapter Four

The Beginning and the End

Menstruation

One thing that is responsible for a great deal of stress for many women is the monthly menstrual cycle. The onset of menstruation, painful periods, what can be done about them, what happens when they come to an end – these are just some of the problems faced from puberty to late middle age.

Of course some women sail through, month after month, with never a pain or a problem – but such fortunate people are few. And even then, things can change. A colleague told me that from the day her periods started, they were so trouble-free that she could never understand what the other girls were going on about when they complained about being in pain or feeling unwell and used this as a reason to avoid physical education lessons at school.

All that changed, however, when she had her first child. Although the labour was relatively easy and she did not need any stitches or experience any problems afterwards, her periods became far more painful and more erratic ever afterwards. Now she understood exactly what her schoolfriends had meant all those years ago.

The onset of periods can bring stresses of its own. Most young girls like to be the same as their friends and, because periods can start at any age from about ten onwards, the likelihood is that there will be a vast discrepancy in starting dates among a group of friends. The late starters may then worry that there is something wrong with them and that they might never be 'normal' or be able to have children of their own.

Because girls are starting to have periods at a younger age now, it is so important they know what is to happen to them. The responsibility for this lies not only with teachers but also with parents. Some teachers are excellent and will inform their pupils of the way their bodies work and what is going to happen in a clear and sensitive way. Others, however, find this extremely difficult and may either impart information in a clinical and factual manner or become too vague and 'airy-fairy' about the whole thing.

If you are going to tell your daughter about the changes in her body she is to expect, make sure that you do it early enough.

Tina was only ten years old when she experienced her first period – and no one in her family had yet explained to her what was going to happen. The whole family – Tina, her parents and her two younger sisters – were on holiday in a cottage they had rented in mid-Wales.

One morning Helen (Tina's mother) awoke to hear the sound of sobbing coming from the room shared by her three daughters. She rushed in to find a distraught Tina in bed and crying while her two little sisters stared at her wide-eyed. Unable to see what was causing the tears, Helen put her arms around Tina who whispered to her mother that she thought she was dying. She had woken up that morning feeling a little uncomfortable, had seen spots of blood on the bottom sheet and had assumed that she was bleeding to death.

Helen told me afterwards that she felt extremely guilty for not having told Tina about periods but it just had not occurred to her that they would begin while the child was still so young.

In another family where there were three girls, the first two began their periods at between 12 and 13 years of age, but their younger sister Sarah showed no signs of starting by her 14th birthday. Sarah was already worried because she knew that most of her friends had started and this was not helped by her older sisters who kept asking her whether she had too. She began to wonder whether there was perhaps something wrong with her, whether she would never have a period and therefore never be able to have a baby.

The more stressed poor Sarah became, the less likely it was that her periods would begin, thus causing her to feel even more wretched. It was only when the variation in age of the onset of periods was explained to her – and the fact that the age at which she began would make no difference to her fertility – that she was able to be more relaxed about the whole thing.

The anxiety Sarah felt actually exacerbated the problem. You probably know that extreme stress can cause any woman to experience changes in her monthly cycle and can even cause her to miss one or more periods altogether.

When anyone – man or woman – is suffering from excess stress, one of the physical occurrences is an increase in the body's production of adrenalin. When a woman produces an excess of adrenalin, there is a reduction in the amount of the female hormones she is able to produce – and this, of course, can lead to both physical and emotional problems.

If you are someone who suffers from erratic or difficult periods or if you frequently have problems with pre-menstrual syndrome, try practising a deep relaxation technique at the relevant times of the month and see whether that makes a difference. In many cases it is all that is needed.

If you experience any sort of difficulty with your menstrual cycle, it is advisable to consult your doctor or a well-woman or similar clinic to ensure that nothing is actually amiss. Once you have ascertained this, there are various self-help methods open to you. You may have to try more than one – or even a combination of several – as different women respond in different ways to the various forms of treatment.

Painful periods

Self-help

- Take aspirin or a similar painkiller (provided you are not allergic to it).
- Practise this simple exercise to help relieve feelings of cramp. Lie on your back with your legs propped up against wall so that they are higher than your head – keep this position for about five minutes (don't get up too quickly or you might feel a little dizzy).
- Take regular gentle exercise throughout your period – just walking would be sufficient.
- Avoid constipation by taking plenty of fluids and eating foods rich in fibre.
- Try taking calcium tablets in the week before you are due to start menstruating, if you regularly suffer from painful periods. The uterus needs calcium if it is to make the contractions which can ease the pain.
- Avoid highly spiced or excessively salty foods both during your period and in the week or so beforehand.
- Take vitamin E capsules to improve circulation in general and the flow of blood to the womb in particular – this can often reduce pain.
- Enlist the aid of a complementary therapist. Acupuncture, hypnotherapy, aromatherapy and osteopathy can all help relieve pain. Homoeopathy and medical herbalism (either Western or Oriental) take a more long-term view and often help in the correction of any hormone imbalance.

Excessively heavy periods

The question here, of course, is what is meant by 'heavy' – different women will have different views on this. A good way of judging is to ask yourself whether your periods are heavy enough to disrupt your life. If they do, you could class them as 'heavy'.

(Should your periods suddenly become heavy, do consult your medical adviser as there may be a particular condition which requires specialized treatment.)

Self-help

- Increase your iron intake to avoid iron deficiency. You can do this by taking iron tablets but many people find that these encourage constipation. Better still, increase the amount of iron-rich foods you eat by having dark-green vegetables, eggs and meat – especially liver.
- Try taking bioflavonoids. Although no specific scientific tests have been done, helpline advisers report that many women have found them beneficial. Bioflavonoids can be taken as a supplement but are also found in those foods which have a high natural vitamin C content.
- Consult a complementary therapist. Acupuncture, homoeopathy, Western or Oriental herbalism and aromatherapy are particularly helpful. You could also consult a clinical nutritionist for advice.

Cessation of periods

I am not referring here to the onset of the menopause but to the case of women whose periods suddenly stop after having been normal. Nor am I referring to pregnancy when the cessation of periods is expected. Because it has been known for pregnancy to occur even when it is thought that all precautions have be taken, do ensure this is not the case before trying any self-help treatments, to avoid endangering a foetus that may be present.

If your periods have suddenly stopped, it is best initially to consult your medical adviser or women's clinic to ensure that there is no problem which needs immediate treatment. Having ruled that out, there are various other causes to consider.

- Both severe shock and prolonged stress can stop ovulation – and periods will therefore cease.
- If you are anaemic, your body may decide that it cannot afford to lose any more blood.
- Being considerably underweight can be the reason why periods never start at all or why they come to a sudden halt – those who suffer from anorexia nervosa or bulimia rarely have regular periods.

Self-help

- Have yourself tested for anaemia if you feel this may be the problem. In extreme cases it is possible to have iron injections, but for most people an increase in the quantity of iron in their food is sufficient.
- Look at your lifestyle and see whether you have been under a great deal of stress lately. If so, practise regular relaxation techniques to ease the situation.
- Seek outside help if you suffer from anorexia or bulimia. Please consider talking to someone who can help you as this situation is often too big for you to deal with on your own.
- Try a complementary therapy. Those which can help include homeopathy, hypnotherapy, acupuncture, Western or Oriental herbalism.

Premenstrual syndrome (PMS)

This can affect women in various ways – both physically and emotionally. Below are some of the most common symptoms.

- pain or discomfort;
- headaches;
- bloated stomach (this can literally be the case or it can be just a sensation);
- rapid mood swings (from being 'high' to extreme – and sometimes violent – rages);
- frequent crying;
- cravings for particular foods, particularly sweet, sugary ones;
- lack of confidence;
- need to pass water more often than usual;
- depression;
- feelings of extreme tension.

Self-help

Because there is no single symptom and no single cause, you will find a variety of self-help suggestions given here. Some of these will suit you while others may not (though they won't make you any worse). Much as I would like to wave a magic wand and tell you exactly which method will be right for you, I can only suggest that you try those which appeal to you and keep a note of the results.

- Talk! Explain to those closest to you what is happening, how it makes you feel and the fact that you need their understanding and support while you try to find a way of easing the situation.
- Ensure that your diet is as healthy as possible during this time. Some women find that they feel better on several small meals a day rather than the usual routine of breakfast, lunch and supper.
- Avoid processed foods and drinks with a high caffeine content.
- Try taking vitamin B$_6$, either as a single supplement or combined with Oil of Evening Primrose.

- Increase the amount of steady exercise you take in the ten days before your period is due. This releases the body's endorphins and this can have a calming effect.
- Make a relaxation technique part of your regular routine – as we have already seen, an increase in adrenalin can inhibit the flow of the female hormones.
- Plan your life carefully until you have managed to get your PMS under control – don't arrange a child's birthday party, an important business meeting, or anything which is likely to cause you excess stress, for your bad days.
- Keep to hand Rescue Remedy from the Bach Flower Remedies – now widely available in health shops and some chemists – and found to be generally beneficial.
- Spoil yourself with a long soak in a warm bath, a glossy magazine, a favourite piece of music – or whatever other indulgence particularly appeals to you.
- Do take the time (at some other time of the month) to explain to your partner that lack of libido can be one of the symptoms of PMS and this may be why you suddenly appear not to want sex – or even, in some cases, to be touched in any way at all.
- Try any of the complementary therapies already recommended in this chapter – they can all be helpful.
- Contact a PMS advisory centre, support group or telephone helpline.

The Menopause

The way in which you view the onset of the menopause depends in part upon the symptoms which you may or may not experience but also – and probably an even greater part – on your mental approach to it.

The positive approach to the menopause is to see it as a time in your life when you no longer have to worry about the possibility of becoming pregnant or to suffer the discomfort or inconvenience of periods. It is a time when you will be able to think more about yourself and what you want to do.

Some women are far more negative about this time of their lives and see it as an ending to their womanliness and the beginning of old age. For most women the menopause usually begins in their late forties or early fifties (although it can begin even earlier) – and very few 50-year-olds would consider themselves to be old these days.

It is recommended that you consider continuing your usual form of birth control for two full years after the date of your last period in order to avoid the stress of a late and unexpected pregnancy – and the equally great stress of wondering whether one will occur.

Don't approach your menopause expecting to have a hard time. In fact, as Nikki Bradford points out in *The Well Woman's Self-Help Directory* (published in association with Marie Stopes Women's Health Clinics): 'according to the US National Institute of Health, 80 per cent of women will experience only mild symptoms, or none at all. Around 20 per cent will have some menopausal symptoms severe enough to need medical help. More good news: for every unwelcome symptom, there is a solution.'

Hormone Replacement Therapy (HRT)

This has become more commonly used and more easily available and can be found in various forms – pills, implants or patches. I do not intend to go into details of the medical aspects here as I am not qualified to do so. Having interviewed many women on this subject – some of whom swear by HRT, others have had unfortunate experiences with it – I would, however, suggest that you seek professional advice on whether or not it would suit you. It is usual then to give it a trial period, during which time you should be kept under supervision. This is because some women react well to one type and badly to another – while about one in five women cannot tolerate HRT at all.

Symptoms and self-help

Hot flushes   These vary from simply feeling that you are growing warmer to actually becoming red-faced and sweating – which can prove to be embarrassing at work or in company. If you experience this, there are various things you can do to help relieve the situation.

- Wear several thin layers of clothing so that you can remove one if necessary; wear clothes made of natural fibres where possible.
- Practise hypnotherapy and breathing exercises to bring quick relief.
- Keep your weight down; body fat acts as an insulating material.
- Keep a small portable fan on your desk or in your handbag.
- Carry a handbag-size facial water spray for instant cooling.

Psychological problems   These can range from feeling that you are growing old to depression and lack of confidence.

- Seek the assistance of a professional counsellor or contact the appropriate helpline.
- Make plans for your future – some may be long term but others you can begin to put into action *now*.
- Try a combination of relaxation and visualization techniques to induce a more positive state of mind. If you find this difficult to achieve alone because you are in a negative state, seek the help of a hypnotherapist or a yoga teacher.
- Maintain a regular exercise pattern as this will send an increased supply of oxygen to the brain, thus allowing you

to think more clearly and rationally and not get over-whelmed by your emotions.

Osteoporosis   This condition affects about one in every four women who have passed the menopause. It can cause you to lose height, to suffer from brittle bones or to develop what is often known as the 'dowager's hump'.

Certain women are more likely to develop osteoporosis. Look at the categories below; if you come into one or more of them, it is worth while having a check-up to find out whether you have early signs of osteoporosis, in which case treatment can usually be offered. Once it passes that early stage, there is usually little that can be done. Most at risk are:

- small, thin women (oestrogen to counteract the condition is formed and stored in fat deposits in the body);
- those who have suffered from anorexia or bulimia;
- women who started their periods late or their menopause early;
- those who have been heavy smokers or heavy drinkers;
- those who take very little regular exercise.

If you fall into one of the above categories, you should seek professional advice as soon as you are aware of your menopause. For others, the following advice may prove helpful.

- Eat sensibly so that you do not put too much strain on your skeleton.
- Exercise regularly as this has been shown to reduce the likelihood of the onset of osteoporosis.
- Stop smoking and keep your alcohol intake at a reasonable level.
- Consider taking calcium in the form of a supplement if you are not getting enough of it in your food.

Hysterectomy

In some cases a hysterectomy is essential in order to relieve a life-threatening condition. In other cases it is only one of a number of choices. You may feel that you would like to consider those other choices before undergoing surgery, so do ensure that you are given all the facts and told of all the options before deciding whether or not to go ahead.

If you talk to women who have had a hysterectomy, you will hear many different reports – both of the operation itself and of the way these women felt afterwards. Speaking personally, I had a total hysterectomy when I was in my thirties (nearly 20 years ago) and I had no problems, either physical or emotional, at the time or since. I do appreciate, however, that it is not the same for everyone.

There are many 'old wives' tales' and groundless fears associated with this operation and unless you are able to separate these from the facts, they will only add to the stress you are feeling. And this will be at a time when you particularly want a clear head so that you can make the best decision for yourself.

These are some of the mistaken ideas surrounding hysterectomy.

- 'If the uterus is removed, there will be an empty space left inside where it should be.' This is not true. Your abdominal organs will move around and fill up any gap.
- 'You will become less feminine and less attractive.' There is no physical reason for this. If you do experience such feelings after the operation, they are psychologically based and you should talk them over with an experienced counsellor.
- 'You will age in appearance and experience all the symptoms of the menopause.' If your ovaries are not removed, this will not happen at all. If they are, you still may not

experience such symptoms (I didn't), but if you do, refer back to the section on the menopause above – you don't have to suffer.

Before the operation

- Find out precisely what is going to happen. There are various types of hysterectomy; it may or may not include the removal of the ovaries and/or the Fallopian tubes. It has been shown that people who understand what is going on suffer less pain and recover more quickly than those who do not. Don't rely only on reading medical books – you will probably frighten yourself more than is necessary. Talk. Talk to your GP, your consultant or an expert from a support group.
- Talk about your feelings too – to your husband or partner, to your family or to a counsellor. Remember that your partner is likely to have his own fears on your behalf, so although this concerns *you* and your body, try not to shut him out.
- Ask for – and practise – the exercises designed to strengthen the muscles of the pelvic floor and the stomach.

After the operation

- Start doing the special exercises again once you have been given permission to do so. Not only will these help to tone up the abdominal muscles they will also help to disperse the wind which often follows this operation.
- Don't be in too much of a hurry to rush around the house or get back to work. You are likely to do yourself more harm than good. You will need a lot of rest for the first week or two – so let everyone else help you.
- Avoid lifting anything at all. Even items that seem quite

light (even a tray with a cup of tea and a plate of biscuits) can impose strain on those internal stitches.

- Start to walk about as soon as you feel able to. Walking is probably the best form of exercise and it will also ensure that your circulation does not suffer. Start by walking for just a few minutes each day and build up gradually. Never do more than is comfortable and ensure that your posture is good as you walk – don't be tempted to bend forwards all the time.
- Avoid the extra strain of constipation by drinking plenty of fluids and eating fibre-rich foods.

Resuming sex

This is an area where there are often any number of fears and anxieties but following the points below should eliminate most of these.

- Don't even consider having intercourse until after your six-week check-up. But this does not mean that you cannot hold, kiss and cuddle your partner as much as you both wish.
- Ensure that you know exactly what has been done. You can do this at the check-up. Ask too whether it is likely to have any effect on your sex life.
- Talk to your partner. Either of you may well feel nervous about starting to have intercourse again. You are not sure what it will feel like, whether it will be 'different', whether you might do any harm. Ideally, armed with your knowledge of the extent of your operation and its likely effects, you will be able to discuss this together. If one or both of you finds this difficult, do seek the help of caring professional who is used to dealing with such matters.
- Try one of the many complementary therapies which can help deal with this problem, and with any other aspect of a hysterectomy.

As in many other aspects of life, an awareness of a situation can greatly reduce any stress which might be associated with it. Whether you are dealing with menstruation, the menopause or a hysterectomy, learn to be in tune with your mind and your body so that you realize what is happening to you at any given time. It is only when you experience such realization that you will do anything to deal with any problems which might arise – and thus reduce the stress from which you would otherwise be suffering.

Chapter Five

Pregnancy and Childbirth

Pregnancy and childbirth are often spoken of as 'the most natural things in the world' – and in one sense perhaps they are. But they are also among the most stressful.

This has always been the case, although the reasons behind that stress may be different now. The further back in time we look, the more dangerous the whole process was. 'Natural', in the days before modern medicine and self-help techniques were available, often equated with 'agonizing' and even 'dangerous'. It was not unusual for women to die or to suffer irreparable damage during labour and many babies did not survive the birth.

Even for those who did, a successful passage through childhood was by no means guaranteed. I can remember women of my grandmother's generation boasting that they had 'borne eight children and raised six'. They were proud of the fact that they had lost only two. This doesn't mean that those poor little ones were not loved – but it was a fact accepted by the majority that there was little likelihood of the entire family reaching adulthood.

The lack of birth control methods, coupled with poverty and its accompanying poor nutrition, made the wear and tear on the mothers of generations past quite dramatic, with many women enduring lives of real hardship and often dying far earlier than they should have.

The problems that exist in the Western world today

may be very different and fewer of them may result in the death of either mother or child – but they are stress-inducing nonetheless.

Is the pregnancy wanted?

With all the education, assistance and information available today, you would think that there need be no such thing as an unwanted pregnancy – and yet they still exist in consider-able numbers. And very few of these are due to mishaps such as faulty contraceptives. Most occur because of a few moments of thoughtlessness or because someone has thought 'it will never happen to me'.

Every year there are numbers of teenage girls who find themselves pregnant. Even if the father stays close (and often he is little more than a boy himself) and even if the girl's own parents are loving and supportive, this can be a time of stress and distress – which is not good for the young expectant mother and certainly not good for her unborn child.

At such times there are so many decisions to be made. Fortunately the stigma of giving birth outside either mar-riage or a permanent and stable relationship is not as great as it was – we no longer shut girls and young women away in mental institutions for having committed the great 'sin' of becoming pregnant. But the choices to be made are many. Should she have an abortion? Should she have the baby adopted or should she keep it? So many options – and each one bringing possible heartache in its wake.

> Lynette was devastated when she discovered that her 14-year-old daughter Katy was pregnant after drinking at a friend's birthday party. Katy knew nothing about her baby's father except his first name; he had been among a group of youths who had gatecrashed the party and she had never seen him before or since.
>
> Distressed as they felt, Lynette and her husband nevertheless wanted to do the best for their daughter – but what was the best?

Was it a good thing physically or emotionally for a 14-year-old girl to go through the entire pregnancy and labour? If she did, what should be done with the baby? Should she keep it and make it far more difficult to continue her studies? Should her parents keep it and try to raise it as their own child? Should it be handed over for adoption to be brought up by a family of strangers?

Then there was the possibility of abortion. Here Lynette had great inner conflict. She had always declared that, except in certain cases of danger to health or severe deformity, she was totally opposed to abortion. But her own child had never before been involved in the situation.

As in all such cases, there was only a limited time in which to make a decision. Katy herself did not know what she wanted. She was an emotionally immature girl who was torn between the idea of being a mother (picturing her baby as some living doll to be played with rather than the demanding infant it would be) and wanting to be free of the whole problem and back to school with her friends.

Eventually, having taken advice from those who were in a position to give it and having discussed it endlessly among themselves, the family – including Katy – came to the conclusion that abortion would be the appropriate course of action in this case.

The abortion was duly carried out and physically all went well. Katy seemed to get over the emotional hurdles quite quickly but, of course, no one can know what will be the long-term effects and how she will feel about it in years to come. Lynette, however, suffered tremendous pangs of guilt after-wards, feeling that she had sacrificed another life in order to make her own daughter's life easier. It took a long time and considerable outside help for her to come to terms with what had happened.

It is not for me to say whether the family's decision was right or not. I have never had to confront such a situation. You will have your own views, but unless you have been in the same position you cannot be certain what you would do in Lynette's situation.

At least Katy had been able to talk to her parents. There are many cases where the girl is so scared of her parents' possible reaction – with or without justification – that she does not tell them of her situation until it is too late for some of the options to be considered. And although there are now far fewer cases of 'never darken my doorstep again', nonetheless not all parents are as understanding and supportive as Lynette and her husband.

Even within a marriage or a permanent relationship, pregnancy is not always wanted. There are still accidents connected with contraception – either a particular method does not work efficiently or (for whatever reason) is not used at all.

I even know of one case where, because of the husband's abnormally low sperm count, a couple were told that there was little possibility of them becoming parents. After some initial distress, the couple had put all thoughts of children from their minds and had gone on to build a successful business and personal relationship which brought them both a great deal of pleasure. Think of their reaction when they discovered that the wife – now in her early forties – was pregnant.

Some women who feel that they may well want children at some time in the future are distressed to find that they are pregnant far sooner than intended. Their stress may be caused by problems of timing – perhaps they are in the middle of some form of vocational training – or finances. Perhaps they do not have anywhere suitable to live and to bring up a child or perhaps they fear that their job will not be kept available for them while they take time off to have and care for their baby.

Most of these problems can be handled – and usually are – in such a way that a solution is reached which, if not entirely satisfactory, is nonetheless bearable. But in reaching such solutions, the woman will have gone through a period of strain just at a time when she should be trying to reduce the stress in her life.

Difficulty in becoming pregnant

For every girl or woman who encounters an unwanted pregnancy, there is another who desperately longs for a baby of her own but, for one reason or another, never becomes pregnant. This situation is made even more stressful when medical examination of both the man and the woman shows that there appears to be no reason why pregnancy should not occur.

One woman in her thirties who had been hoping for over ten years to become pregnant told me that she felt 'inadequate' and 'a failure'. Everywhere she looked she seemed to see young women producing child after child while she could not even conceive once. She became very bitter when she heard of teenage girls becoming pregnant, of the increasing number of abortions performed and of parents handing their children over for adoption. Her own inability to conceive coloured her whole existence. She was unable to think of anything else and it eventually endangered her relationship with her husband – who was just as anxious for a family as she was.

I'm happy to say that after help from various complementary therapists and an organization called Foresight (see page 71), this particular woman went on to give birth to two healthy boys.

In a case where a woman does not become pregnant even though there are no physical reasons for this, she is usually advised to do what she can to reduce the amount of stress in her life. But what a difficult task she is being set! It is this failure to conceive which is actively responsible for a great deal of that stress. And this problem becomes more stressful the older she gets and the more she is aware of her biological clock ticking away.

Because physical, mental and emotional relaxation is so important at such a time, it is well worth seeking outside help in order to achieve it. Some women derive great benefit from yoga, some from meditation techniques. As a hypnothera-pist, I have worked over the years with dozens of would-be mothers, teaching them forms of deep relaxation and helping them deal with the accumulated emotional stress – and I can recall only one or two who failed to become pregnant within a year of commencing treatment.

There are also many instances of beneficial help being derived from treatment by acupuncture, homeopathy, aromatherapy and herbalism – both Western and, in particu-lar, Oriental. You may feel, therefore, that it is worth trying one or more of these therapies in combination with relaxation techniques.

If you have been experiencing difficulty in conceiving, you might try following these guidelines – and remember that they apply to both the man and the woman.

- Stop smoking. Quite apart from the obvious health bene-fits, a study by the US National Institute of Environmental Health Sciences in 1985 found that women who smoke are three times less likely to conceive than those who do not. In addition, the sperm count of men who smoke is likely to be lower than that of men who do not. (This applies to both tobacco and any other smoked substances.)
- Stop drinking alcohol until conception has taken place – and, when it has, women should try to abstain for the first three months of pregnancy.
- Follow a healthy diet, incorporating raw and whole-foods. If you are not sure what constitutes a healthy diet for you, contact a nutritional therapist for advice on this and on whether you are in need of any vitamin or mineral supplements.
- Don't worry too much about making love at a specified time in your cycle – you will probably be advised at the time of ovulation, but a day or two on either side can prove just as effective. And don't let this stop you having sex with your partner at other times too – the need to perform

according to the calendar can seem mechanical and can in itself cause distress.

- Take regular exercise but don't overdo it. It is better to take light exercise on a regular basis than to exhaust yourself by pounding the pavement or working out once or twice a week.
- Contact Foresight, an organization dedicated to helping couples with their pre-conceptual care. You will find their address at the back of this book.

Planning for the birth

Even when you are happily pregnant, there are still so many things to think about and so much potential stress around you. If you can, it is as well to make some basic decisions as early on as possible rather than spending months when you should be concentrating on your baby trying to decide what it is you really want.

Let's think about the birth itself. Would you prefer to have it at home or in hospital? What do you feel about such things as forceps deliveries, Caesarean sections, epidurals, gas and air? In an emergency, I am sure you will do whatever is necessary to provide the best labour for yourself and your baby, but it is as well to learn about all the options and decide well in advance which of them you would prefer to be used and which should be kept only as a last resort.

If you would prefer to use complementary painkilling techniques such as acupuncture or hypnotherapy, make your feelings clear as early as possible – both to your medical consultant and the therapist. Acupuncturists and hypnotherapists both like to begin treating the mother some time before the birth – and will, in fact, probably work with her throughout her pregnancy.

A hypnotherapist will teach you self-hypnosis techniques

that you can use during labour. I also like to give my patients an individually-made cassette to ensure that they relax and breathe properly at appropriate times while the labour is taking place. In these days of personal stereos, the mother can take the cassette into the labour room with her and have my voice and words to concentrate on. (Needless to say, there is always a proviso built into the wording on the cassette so that, should an emergency arise, the instructions of a doctor or midwife will always take precedence over those on the tape.)

> Some years ago I was consulted by Sonia, the 40-year-old mother of two teenage boys. Sonia suddenly found herself pregnant again and, although it had not been planned, she was overjoyed. However, she had not had an easy time during the birth of either of her sons and she was worried that, being considerably older, she would have problems during her forth-coming labour.
>
> I worked with Sonia throughout her pregnancy, teaching her self-hypnosis so that she could use it at any time. This was also the first time I had ever made a cassette for one of my patients to use during labour itself.
>
> Shortly afterwards I received a letter from Sonia telling me that, far from experiencing the difficulties she had when her sons were born, she was able to relax completely between contractions and had actually been able to enjoy the birth of her baby daughter.

First-time pregnancy

However much a baby is wanted and however happy a woman is at finding herself pregnant, there are still many fears and anxieties to be faced and these can be the cause of a great deal of stress. This is particularly so because a woman may not like to admit to anyone that these fears and anxieties actually exist. After all, women have been having babies since the beginning of the human race and she may feel that it is foolish to express her worries.

No matter how many books you read, how many videos you watch or how many pre-natal classes you attend, you can never really know what labour is like until you have experienced it. But of one thing you can be sure – there will always be someone around who will be only too ready to tell you of her agony, of all the things that went wrong, of how long her labour lasted and how she went on suffering for weeks afterwards and 'has never been the same since'.

Try as we might to ignore these prophetesses of doom – and even though many others tell us of the joy of their own experience of childbirth – it is always the fearful images that come into our minds when we are feeling tired or fed up. If you are a newly pregnant woman and this is to be your first child, you might like to bear in mind that, complain as they might, most of these women went on to bear subsequent children. Would they have done so if the whole process had been the hell they describe?

It is not only fear of childbirth itself which induces stress in a woman who is pregnant for the first time. Every new sensation, every new movement feels strange and a hundred questions fill her mind. 'Is this what it is supposed to feel like?', 'Shouldn't the baby be kicking by now?', 'Does this pain in my back mean that something is going wrong?'

As the date you have been given for the birth approaches, you wonder what it will be like and whether you will know when it has started. For those women whose waters do not break at the outset, every twinge and every movement can seem like indications of the first contraction. At the time when you need to be as calm as possible, you may well be sitting on the edge of your seat, suitcase by your feet, feeling the tension growing as your fingers edge nearer and nearer to the telephone.

During pregnancy

Some women seem to sail happily through their pregnancy with nothing but their increasing girth to indicate what is happening within them. An unfortunate few experience real health problems, great or small. The majority, however, cope fairly well – possibly experiencing some sickness in the first weeks but little else of significance until the end of the pregnancy approaches.

But even among these women, there are many minor irritations and inconveniences to add to their stress level – from indigestion to swollen ankles, from food cravings or loathings to backache. None of these problems is a major one but any or all can be sufficient to cause undue stress. Add to this the fact that a fluctuation in hormone levels may already be causing mood swings – sometimes quite dramatic ones – and you will see why some women find it very difficult to relax.

A little knowledge . . .

When I was expecting my sons there were no scans or tests during pregnancy for Downs syndrome. Some women did not even know they were going to give birth to more than one baby until it happened. One acquaintance of mine was told by the doctor who was attending her, 'You have a lovely little girl', only to hear him say a few moments later, 'Oh, you have another lovely little girl.' The twins had been lying in such a way in her womb that only one heartbeat had been audible.

It is obvious that the availability of scans and tests can give a good deal of information and can help put minds at rest – but they can also cause stress too.

One of my patients, Angie, came to me in a state of great distress when she was about six months pregnant. She had been feeling fine, having got over her initial morning sickness, and was looking forward greatly to the birth of her baby (she already had two young children). A recent scan, however, had shown an unusual mark and Angie and her husband were told to be prepared for the fact that there might be something wrong with one of the baby's kidneys. No one could be sure, they were told, until the baby was born and tests were carried out.

The remainder of the pregnancy was very difficult for Angie – however hard she tried to think positively. After all, she had been told that even if there was a kidney defect and even if one looked at the worst possible scenario, most people can manage perfectly well with only one kidney. But just the thought of her tiny, newborn infant having to be poked and prodded as tests were undertaken was difficult for Angie to cope with. Having two other young children to care for, her days were well occupied and she had little time for thinking, but her mind raced over all the possibilities and the long-term effects they might have for the entire family. She was finding it difficult to sleep at night and was, therefore, becoming tired and irritable during the day. Fortunately I was able to teach her an advanced form of self-hypnosis which allowed her some respite from her anxious thoughts.

The baby was born; the tests were carried out – and there proved to be nothing at all wrong with either of the infant's kidneys. No explanation was found for the odd-shaped stain on the scan but at least they now knew that the baby was perfectly fit and well.

Scans and tests can be so helpful – and, anyway, it is not possible to retreat from progress. However, in this particular case, far from reducing the amount of stress felt by Angie and her husband, this modern technology had actually served to increase it.

Pre-birth communication

One of the things it is possible to do by means of hypnosis is to take an individual back to the time when he or she was still in the womb.

This is usually done when trying to find the initial cause for the onset of a phobia when a child appears to have been born with one.

> A former patient suffered from both claustrophobia and recurrent migraine. However far we took her back in her childhood, those symptoms appeared to have been present. She could even recall under hypnosis how she would scream in panic if the hood was raised on her pram.
>
> It turned out that this woman's mother had unfortunately suffered two miscarriages and had had minor surgery to close up the neck of the womb during pregnancy so that the baby could not be born too early. The unborn child – who later became my patient – could recall attempting to find a way out of this place but, of course, this was now impossible – hence the onset of her claustrophobia. In addition, having turned in preparation for being born, the baby repeatedly banged her head against the wall of the womb as she attempted to escape – hence the migraine.

Babies in the womb are also extremely sensitive to the feelings of the mother and the atmosphere in which they find themselves. They may not understand words but they certainly know whether the atmosphere is happy, sad, frightened, or angry (this can be ascertained by regressing someone to that period before birth).

This is one of the reasons that I always spend time with mothers-to-be who come to consult me, encouraging them and helping them to communicate with their unborn child. If a woman can set aside a period of time each day to do nothing but relax with her baby and talk to it, it is beneficial for both of them. It doesn't matter whether the words are spoken aloud or whether they are thoughts in the mother's head – the baby will understand the feelings behind them.

Imagine how good it must feel if some part of every day is given over to surrounding you with thoughts of love and caring – could any baby want a better start? And, of course, it is good for the mother too. Not only is she enjoying a period of physical relaxation, but she is concentrating on the positive aspects of her pregnancy. And by reinforcing and re-emphasizing her love for her unborn child, she knows that she is giving their future relationship the best possible start.

If you decide to put this into practice – and I truly hope that you will – you might like to choose an appropriate piece of music to play gently in the background as you do so. This should preferably be music without words – the words might distract you and you might find yourself listening to them rather than concentrating on the baby within you.

It has also been found that if the same piece of music is used every time you have this peaceful and loving period with your baby, the child will often react to it as a lullaby in the future. This isn't really surprising when you think that he or she has come to associate that particular piece of music with a time when all is warm and comfortable and the mother's body is really relaxed.

Complementary therapies

There are many ways in which complementary therapies can be useful in counteracting the physical and emotional stresses of pregnancy and childbirth.

The majority of therapists will want to see a woman at regular intervals throughout her pregnancy. Apart from the actual benefits received from the treatment, stress is greatly reduced for most women because they are able to consult someone who has time to spend with them, helping and advising them during what is one of the most important periods of their life. It is also good to know that whatever treatment your therapist decides is appropriate for you, it will have been worked out for you personally, based on an extensive examination of your history. You will not be treated as 'a pregnant woman'; you will be treated as an individual with a physical and emotional background which is different to that of any other woman.

The therapies most beneficial at such times are:

- acupuncture;
- hypnotherapy;
- Western or Oriental herbalism;
- aromatherapy;
- nutrition;
- homoeopathy.

Each of these can have a role to play and it is for you to decide which type of therapist you would prefer to consult. For your further help and information, a contact address for each therapy will be found at the end of this book.

A woman may suffer many stresses in connection with pregnancy and childbirth but – armed with information, outside help if necessary and techniques to make things easier – the majority of these stresses can be reduced or even overcome.

Chapter Six

The Distressing Side of Pregnancy

Pregnancy should be a time of joyous anticipation. Even though there may be attendant discomforts, for most women this is a very happy time as they look forward to the birth of their baby. But for some – and probably more than is realized – pregnancy turns out to be a painful time, a time of anxiety and certainly of stress.

Miscarriage

It is estimated that about one in six women who have had their pregnancy confirmed will suffer a miscarriage – and if you take into account very early miscarriages when the woman may not even realize that she is pregnant, this number rises to one in three.

A pregnancy which terminates spontaneously before the 24th week is termed a miscarriage, while one which occurs after that time is technically a stillbirth. Many medical practitioners still use the term 'spontaneous abortion' to describe what you and I think of as a miscarriage. Even though this is the correct term, the word 'abortion' can cause a great deal of stress in a woman who has just been through a very distressing experience.

The first thing any woman in such a situation thinks is likely to be 'Why me?' But often there can be no clear answer.

In about six cases out of ten a definite – or at least probable – explanation can be given. In the remaining four cases, however, no one is able to determine the cause.

This leaves many women wondering whether they perhaps did something wrong to cause the miscarriage. In addition, they may feel totally helpless because if they do not know what went wrong, there is nothing they can do differently next time to ensure the same thing will not happen again.

There are, of course, some excellent doctors around who take time to talk to their patients and who really feel for them in times of distress. But there are also many of the other kind who show no compassion when dealing with a woman who has just suffered a miscarriage. Through the local branch of the Miscarriage Association, I have worked with many such women of all ages and the majority of them have been shown little sensitivity by those who have treated them.

'Just think of it as a heavy period' one young woman was told by her GP soon after she lost her baby in the fourth month of her pregnancy. But that wasn't a heavy period – it was her child. The fact that it was not yet completely developed didn't alter that fact. She had suffered a bereavement, not a particularly uncomfortable menstruation.

In these days when counselling is available to help people overcome so many traumas in their lives, I find it amazing that none exists for women who have just experienced one of the most distressing events imaginable. In most areas, were it not for organizations like the Miscarriage Association, there would be nowhere at all for these women to go. At the Association's meetings, however, they are able to talk together, to cry if they need to, to support each other and to gain hope by hearing of former members who have gone on to experience successful pregnancies and the birth of one or more children.

At whatever stage of the pregnancy the miscarriage takes place, to the woman concerned – and to some extent to a supportive partner – this is a bereavement and should be treated as such. This means that all the normal stages of bereavement need to be experienced.

By saying that the supportive partner only feels this as a bereavement 'to some extent' is not intended to belittle the very real grief and pain a caring husband or partner may feel. But whereas in a case of early infant mortality or a cot death, he has had a chance to see and touch the child, at the time of a miscarriage he cannot possibly have had the same experience as the mother within whom the baby was growing.

If you experience the death of any loved person of any age, there are certain generally acknowledged stages you have to go through. You will realize this and so will others. Yet with a miscarriage the woman is often expected to 'get over it' quite quickly and other people expect her to be 'back to normal' very soon afterwards. Indeed, in many cases she expects this of herself and so does not allow herself time to experience the stages of bereavement.

The most significant of these stages are grief, anger and guilt.

Grief

Any mother will grieve for the loss of her unborn child – and people will expect her to do so. Yet whereas it is accepted that one may grieve for a considerable period of time for a person who has lived, somehow – perhaps because no one but the mother ever really knew the baby – this particular form of grief is supposed to be put behind her quite quickly. When this is not possible, the mother may well begin to blame herself or feel that there is something wrong with her because she is not living up to what other people expect of her.

When someone dies we usually mark their passing with a service, a burial or a cremation. We talk about them with others who have known them. We have photographs to look at and memories to recall. When you lose someone who has not yet been born, those things are not possible. But there are things you can do which will serve the same purpose.

• If it was a late miscarriage, it is still sometimes possible to arrange a burial. If this is what you want, you must make your views clear to the doctor or hospital. (If you do not feel up to making such requests or arrangements yourself, ask a caring friend or relative to do so on your behalf.)

• Give your baby a name. This is acknowledging to yourself and to the world that this was a real person and not just some temporary 'illness'. It also stops you having to refer to your unborn son or daughter as 'it' which can be upsetting. (If the miscarriage took place before you were able to discover the sex of the child, allow your intuition to tell you which it was.)

• Have a tangible object, bought specifically for this baby, to remind you of his or her existence. It doesn't matter what this is provided it is significant to you. One couple I know planted a bed of roses in their garden. A young woman bought a teddy bear which she kept in her bedroom. This is not a morbid exercise but a way of allowing yourself to grieve for a person who lived – albeit briefly and only inside your body.

• Remember your partner who will be grieving too. Just because he has not experienced the child in the way that you have does not mean that his grief is not real. Indeed, if he is sensitive enough to realize that he can never feel the same as you do about the loss, he may well find it difficult to know what to say or do. So include him in your grieving process and your relationship will be the richer for it.

Anger

The anger we feel after a bereavement is not necessarily logical – but it is natural. There could be anger at life in general, at a god who could allow this to happen, at the doctor who did not know this was going to happen, at other mothers for having healthy babies, at women who have abortions or give birth only to hand their child over for adoption. There can be anger at the sun for shining, the birds for singing and the flowers for blooming.

Because this anger seems wrong to us – and particularly what appear to be the more illogical aspects of it – we often try and suppress it. But this is harmful. Don't try to analyse *why* you feel angry; just accept that it is a normal part of any bereavement. Acknowledge your feelings and the intensity and frequency of the anger will soon diminish.

Guilt

Guilt after any bereavement is perfectly natural, but perhaps it causes more torment to the sufferer after a miscarriage than at almost any other time – except perhaps after the tragedy of a cot death.

It doesn't matter how many times an expectant mother is told that the loss of her unborn child was not her fault, there will always be a part of her which wonders whether she did too much, lifted something too heavy, didn't take sufficient care with her diet – or any other of a million possibilities.

Possibly the greatest sense of guilt arises when the woman knows that she did not really want the baby in the first place – whether she has ever expressed that view to anyone or not.

Cathy was 26 when she discovered she was pregnant. Although they did not live together, Bill had been her constant partner for nearly four years. They had often talked about getting married and having a family – but this was always an idea for some distant time in the future.

Cathy worked for one of the major oil companies and, two months before finding that she was pregnant, she was promoted to the job of her dreams. She was one of the youngest people –

male or female – to attain this level of seniority and the job carried with it all sorts of perks, such as frequent international travel, a beautiful top-of-the-range car and an extremely high salary.

Because she and Bill had always used contraception, Cathy had no idea how she had become pregnant – but she had. She was devastated and temporarily considered having an abortion, but morally and ethically this was something she felt she could not do. She did not dare mention her condition at work as she knew her employers were not the type to make life easy for her and that they would find some way not to keep her position open for her while she took maternity leave.

When Bill found out about the baby, he was totally supportive and suggested that he and Cathy should marry straight away. He ran a successful business of his own so there would be no financial worries whether Cathy continued to work or not. He could not understand why Cathy did not seem enthusiastic at the prospect.

Cathy felt trapped – imprisoned by the new life growing within her. Each night, as she lay in bed, she would wish that she could turn the clock back to a time before she was pregnant – a time when her life had seemed happy and exciting. But there was nothing she could do.

As the first months passed, a change began to take place in Cathy. She became accustomed to the idea of becoming a mother and began to wonder about her baby and what he or she would be like. Somehow the future did not now appear so bleak and she began to think about telling her employers of her condition.

Apart from a little morning sickness in the first few weeks, Cathy had felt extremely well throughout the early months of her pregnancy. But one day, just after returning home from a trip to the United States, she had a sudden pain, a loss of blood and a terrible sense of foreboding. She sent for the doctor and he confirmed what she had guessed – she had miscarried her baby.

Cathy was given a D and C (dilation and curettage) and suffered no physical ill-effects from the miscarriage. But she was totally unprepared for the grief which overwhelmed her when she thought about her loss. She had expected to simply get on with her life and her work and to feel a sense of relief that she had not yet informed her employers that she was pregnant.

But she was desolate at the loss of this tiny life and tormented herself with guilt by reminding herself how often she had said and thought that she did not want this child – that it was a nuisance and would interfere with her fulfilling existence and her exciting job. She wondered whether these thoughts could in some way have caused the miscarriage. Soon her energy level dropped and she found it difficult either to work or to sleep.

It took several months – during which she was helped by both her doctor and a counsellor – for Cathy to be her old self again. But she was not quite her old self. This Cathy was more contemplative than the old one had been and thought more about what she really wanted from life. She did not feel ready yet for another attempt at motherhood but she did move in with Bill and, while enjoying the job she did, decided that it was something she did not want to do for ever. The following year the couple married and, two years after that, their daughter Chloe was born.

Recognizing a miscarriage

When a woman is experiencing her first pregnancy everything is new to her. Feelings – both physical and emotional – are often different to those she has experienced before. Some women are happy just to allow themselves to experience all these feelings – even those which are a little uncomfortable – and to accept them as a natural part of their pregnancy. Others, however, are frightened of whatever is different and wonder whether each new sensation is a warning of something terrible which is about to happen.

This does not occur only in a first pregnancy. No two pregnancies – even in the same woman – are identical. Just because you were sick with one child (or developed sciatica or had particular cravings), it does not follow that you will react in the same way with another. This can cause worry because you wonder whether these different feelings mean that something is going wrong this time.

There are various recognized symptoms of a threatened miscarriage and should you experience any of them you should go to bed and send for your doctor. But this is a precaution and do bear in mind that experiencing one of these symptoms does not make it inevitable that a miscarriage will follow.

- bleeding, especially if the blood is clotted ('spotting' in the early days does not necessarily indicate a miscarriage);
- back pain;
- abdominal pain;
- pain similar to that experienced during a period.

Helping yourself

If you experience any of the above and while you are waiting for your doctor or for the results of any tests he or she might suggest, do your best to relax as much as possible. I know that this will be difficult because worry causes tension and naturally you will be worried. But remember that stress and tension cause you to tighten your muscles and increase your pulse rate and blood pressure – none of which will be good for the baby.

Lie down, covering yourself with something warm (but don't be tempted to place a hot-water bottle over your abdomen) and relax as much as you can. If you have been taught a relaxation technique or have a cassette you can use, so much the better. Breathe deeply and slowly and visualize everything being right with the baby within you. While this cannot be guaranteed to avert an impending miscarriage, it will certainly give both you and the baby the best possible chance.

Stillbirth

To lose the baby at any stage of pregnancy is distressing, but it is often even harder for the woman who has carried her child for five or six months. By that time there may have been discussion about names or decoration of a nursery – the type of thing which makes the baby seem more of a person. Suddenly there is no baby – there is no person – and the decorated room is empty and bare.

At this stage it is even more important to name your child and to give it a proper burial or a memorial which conforms with your particular customs and beliefs. Many hospitals will offer the chance of a photograph of the baby; although at first this might seem a morbid thought, many women have found it extremely comforting to have a lasting memento of the tiny, brief life.

Pregnancy after a miscarriage or stillbirth

Even if you have been given an explanation for the loss of your unborn child, and even if it was as a result of a set of circumstances which are unlikely to reoccur, you are bound to approach your next pregnancy with a certain amount of trepidation.

This anxiety can cause you a great deal of stress – and that stress can have a direct and harmful bearing on the pregnancy itself. Now there is no point in telling someone who has miscarried one child and who is expecting another that she shouldn't worry. Of course she will – however much she tries to put the anxieties out of her mind. But by following a basic stress-control routine and by practising relaxation techniques repeatedly, it is possible to ensure that the stress felt does not do any actual harm to mother or child.

If you have suffered one or more miscarriages, it is possible to ask for an ultrasound scan when you are about six weeks into your next pregnancy. It is said that provided the foetus is doing well at this stage, there is only a 5 per cent chance of a miscarriage occurring.

Many women also like to ask for an ultrasound scan about two weeks after the stage at which the miscarriage occurred in the earlier pregnancy. It can be immensely reassuring to know that everything is normal at this stage.

In Chapter 10 you will find many ways in which you can reduce the harmful effects of stress in your life. These apply to all women, not just those who are pregnant – but they are of even greater significance to the latter. Without being fanatical about it, try to follow as many of the suggestions contained there.

There are, in addition, several points to bear in mind when you are pregnant – particularly if you have already suffered one or more miscarriages. You will reduce much of the stress and anxiety if you know for certain that you are doing all you can to maintain a healthy lifestyle for you and your unborn child.

- Stop smoking if you can. Women who smoke during pregnancy are twice as likely to experience a miscarriage. They can also do harm not only to themselves but to the unborn child too. If you are serious about wanting a healthy child, do your best to refrain from smoking altogether, but at the very least, reduce smoking to the minimum amount.
- Reduce your alcohol consumption. In some women even a couple of alcoholic drinks a week can increase the likelihood of a miscarriage. It is wise, therefore, to cut down on alcohol if you can.
- Avoid lifting heavy weights or standing for any length of time.
- Listen to your body and rest when you feel you need to. In some cases, taking long rest periods (actually lying down) at the point in your pregnancy when the previous miscarriage occurred can be beneficial.

- Make sure that the food you eat is properly cooked and avoid any dish which makes use of raw eggs (mayonnaise, etc.) It is also best to avoid such foods as soft cheeses, pâté or anything which could be a breeding ground for salmonella.
- Make sure that your doctor, pharmacist or complementary therapist knows that you are pregnant before accepting any medication or treatment for any other condition.
- Take frequent breaks if you work at a VDU. There is quite a fierce debate as to whether working for many hours at a computer screen can contribute to a miscarriage. The VDU Workers Rights Campaign say: 'Women who work more than 20 hours a week on VDUs are twice as likely to miscarry, according to a major USA research review in 1989.'

Acknowledging your feelings

If you do have the misfortune to suffer the tragedy of miscarriage or stillbirth, allow yourself to work through all the emotions which are part of that event. It is never a good thing to stifle feelings or pretend that all is well and you are over it when you know this is not the case.

Hopefully you will have people close to you to whom you can talk about your feelings. Your partner is the ideal person because he is affected too. But in some cases there is no partner on the scene; in others he may not be able to discuss emotions at any time – particularly now.

> Suzy and Clive had been hoping for a baby for some time and were delighted when Suzy discovered she was pregnant. Sadly, in the fourth month of her pregnancy, Suzy suffered a miscarriage for which no one could find a cause.
>
> After a few days rest and a D and C, Suzy was physically well again but, of course, the emotional trauma took far longer to deal with.

Suzy and Clive hardly discussed the miscarriage and how they felt about it. Each was trying desperately hard to be positive and to spare the other's feelings. Knowing how much she was hurting, Suzy was doing what she could to save Clive experiencing the same pain. So she tried desperately hard to be her old bright self and talk positively about the family they would have in the future. For his part, Clive wanted to help his wife 'get over' the miscarriage and thought that any mention of the baby they had lost would prolong the painful process.

Each of them was acting out of love and concern for the other, but by shutting out their feelings they were making the whole situation far more difficult. Suzy and Clive had to learn to talk to each other, to cry together and to support each other before they were able to contemplate the future with any sense of hope and positivity.

A wound doesn't heal unless it is cleaned and treated; if you just put a plaster over it and hope for the best, it will fester away beneath the dressing. Similarly, we can't come to terms with any situation by pretending that nothing has happened and that everything is just as it was.

If there is no one close to you – friend or family – to whom you can talk about your feelings, do go and see a counsellor or therapist who will be able to help you deal with your emotions and help you come to terms with what has happened.

Chapter Seven

Motherhood

After the birth

Let's imagine an ideal scenario: you've recently given birth to your first child – a perfect and beautiful baby – you have a strong marriage and your husband is being totally support-ive, you have no particular financial worries. Everything in life seems to be wonderful. So why do you feel so dreadful?

You may find yourself feeling frightened, insecure, nerv-ous, unattractive, unhappy. And the fact that you know you should not be experiencing such feelings means that you can add guilt to that list.

It doesn't even help to know that, at any one time, there are literally hundreds of new mothers feeling the same way. For the moment, even if you could bring yourself to believe that fact, you do not care about all those other mothers and their babies; you have enough trouble trying to work out how you are going to cope with your own.

If we look at the areas which seem to be causing you the greatest anxiety, perhaps we can analyse and understand what you are feeling and find a way of dealing with the situation.

Fear of taking care of the baby

This is, naturally, most common after the birth of a first child because being a mother is a completely new experience for you. But it can occur after the birth of a second or subsequent child because even though you may have learned to change a nappy or give a bottle, you have never before learned to cope with a family of two (or three, or more) children at the same time.

However many classes she may have attended and however many books she has read, the new mother probably has not had a chance to put into practice any of the skills at which she is suddenly expected to be an expert. Suddenly there is this tiny, demanding – and often noisy – infant and she is supposed to know exactly what it is that he wants.

What should she do when he cries? Should she pick him up and give him a cuddle – or would that be spoiling him? Should she leave him to cry – or would that be neglect? Is he crying because he is hungry, thirsty, too hot, too cold? Suppose there is something really wrong with him and he is in dreadful pain – how is she to know?

As with any other skill, the more opportunity there is to practise, the easier it gets. And practice is something the new mother is certainly going to have – day after day. Eventually, experience will tell her whether her baby is crying for food, because he is uncomfortable – or whether he is just having a temper tantrum.

However much you love your baby, there will be times when he will infuriate you – perhaps when you are woken up for the third time in one night or when he refuses to take his feed. Then you are likely to feel guilty for being angry with such a little infant who has no way of explaining his wants and needs. You may even be afraid that you might lose your temper and harm your baby – however much the idea repels you.

If you are a new mother filled with such anxieties, until you feel reasonably confident with your baby, don't be afraid to ask for help – whether from a friend or relative who has already brought up children of her own, from your health visitor or from your local mother and baby clinic.

Fears that are not confronted and dealt with are a great cause of stress. The stress, in turn, is likely to increase your sense of fatigue and lead to yet more stress. Anyone who is both tired and under great pressure is likely to lose their sexual desire; should the reasons for this not be understood by your partner, it can prove to be a source of even more friction.

Feeling unattractive

Many physical changes occur during pregnancy – not just the obvious one of the ever-growing bulge – and it may take a little while after the birth for these changes to disappear.

Because the baby will take what it needs in the way of vitamins and minerals, the mother may become depleted. This is why it is so important to follow a healthy regime during pregnancy. Otherwise, hair can become lank and greasy or dry with split ends, and skin which has hitherto never known a blemish may temporarily erupt in a series of spots.

It may take longer than you think to regain your figure and lose any extra weight you put on during the pregnancy. And while some women are delighted with the change in the shape of their bust while breast-feeding, for those who were already amply endowed, it can be a source of misery.

Please don't take all these comments as an ill omen of what is bound to happen. While one or more of them may apply to any woman, it is very unusual for one woman to experience all of them. And the changes are transient; given time and a little care you should soon be the lively and energetic person you once were.

The trouble is that it is very hard to see the shining light at the end of the tunnel when you feel frumpy and unattractive. In the meantime it is only too easy to act as an unattractive woman – someone whose confidence is at a low ebb and who, because she feels unattractive in herself, cannot believe that anyone else would find her desirable. You can see how this could have a devastating result on any relationship – a woman who feels that she is not desirable is likely to act as though this is in fact so and this will be picked up by her partner who may then end up treating her as though she actually is unattractive. And so a vicious circle may be set up.

If you can just accept the fact that any or all of these changes are completely normal and comparatively short-lasting, you should find the whole situation less stressful. Meanwhile, do what you can in the midst of your new and busy regime to find time for yourself. Make sure that you follow a sensible eating pattern – particularly while breast-feeding – and take any supplements which may be necessary. Try and find someone to take care of the baby while you go to the hairdresser, the gym or the swimming pool. And, most important of all, tell your partner how you feel. Even if he cannot empathize completely, friction can perhaps be prevented if he can understand why you are acting in this way.

Feeding

The current school of thought is that breast-feeding is definitely best for the baby – and in the majority of cases this is probably so. But it does not come naturally and easily to every new mother and it can be very frustrating to find either that you do not produce sufficient milk or that your baby does not appear to be thriving on what you do produce. And, of course, the more tense you become about the situation, the less milk you are likely to produce.

Some women, on the other hand, produce so much milk that even when they express some of it, they are constantly troubled by tender breasts or stained blouses.

Margaret was delighted at the birth of her baby son and determined to do her very best to give him a good start in life. Throughout the pregnancy she had taken care of herself and her unborn child, being careful about her diet and following the instructions given to her by her doctor and at the ante-natal clinic.

The baby weighed nearly 8lb at birth and during her short stay in hospital, Margaret was shown how to breast-feed him. Finding this somewhat awkward at first, she continued to receive help and advice from her health visitor when she went home.

Try as she might, Margaret never really felt at ease with breast-feeding. Her breasts became tender and sore and her baby cried at every feed time. And although he seemed to spend a long time at the breast, he was not gaining weight as satisfactorily as he should.

But believing that she was doing her best for her son, Margaret persevered until she could stand it no longer. She ran for help to the mother and baby clinic at her doctor's surgery.

When she was examined it was found that she had abcesses on both breasts and when the baby was test-weighed before and after feeding, it was found that he was only receiving a fraction of what he should. This was the reason for his failure to gain weight and also for the fact that he cried so much – he was hungry.

It was suggested to Margaret that she change to giving her baby a recommended milk by bottle and give up, certainly for the time being, attempting to breast-feed him. Although she realized that this would be sensible, for both their sakes, Margaret couldn't help feeling upset at not being able to feed her child herself. She felt as if she was letting him down in some way.

As time passed, however, she came to see that the combination of happy, well-fed baby and contented and pain-free mother was the sensible solution. Her feelings of guilt and distress disappeared as she watched her little boy thrive.

Although breast-feeding is recommended in as many cases as possible, you may need to accept the fact that it is not for you and that you are not letting your baby down in any way if you find yourself unable to cope with it – for whatever reason.

The really important thing for both of you – whether you feed your child by breast or by bottle – is the closeness and contentedness which should always be part of mealtimes. Even if you are giving a bottle, you can still hold your baby and speak gently to him so that the two of you are able to form a truly close bond. Let feeding time be special, loving and peaceful and you will be giving your baby a wonderful start in life – however you feed him.

Post-natal depression

It has been estimated that about 50 per cent of women experience some form of post-natal depression – but when you are going through it yourself, statistics are of little comfort.

Post-natal depression can vary widely from woman to woman. For some it is quite mild and lasts for just a few days – often being known as 'baby blues'. For others it is a severe condition; these women can experience quite debilitating symptoms over a period of several months.

If the bad news is that it is so common, the good news is that – in almost every case – post-natal depression passes completely. Those women for whom post-natal depression seems to last for a much longer time – even for years – are usually those who have suffered from some sort of depressive or anxiety-related condition before they became pregnant. But they too can be helped.

Mild post-natal depression, which is experienced by many, seems to take the form of tearfulness coupled with a general fear about caring for the baby. This usually passes spontaneously after a day or two.

The symptoms of severe post-natal depression are more varied, the most common being:

- feeling unable to cope;
- inability to eat or sleep well;
- a constant sense of anxiety;
- exhaustion;
- fear of harming the baby.

The most important thing, if you suffer from severe post-natal depression, is to ask for help as soon as possible. No one is going to think any the less of you because you are suffering in this way. You could contact your doctor, the health visitor or the Association for Post-Natal Illness (details in back of book).

Many of the complementary therapies are also highly beneficial in combating the effects of severe post-natal depression. Particularly good results have been achieved through herbal medicine, hypnotherapy and acupuncture, while benefits are also obtained from aromatherapy and homoeopathy.

There are also many ways in which you can help yourself but these should be in addition to, rather than instead of, any outside help you are receiving.

It is really important to talk about how you are feeling – bottling everything up will only make you feel worse and prolong the condition. It is only too easy for anyone who is suffering from any form of depression to feel isolated and 'different' and therefore to be hesitant about telling others how they feel. But people – and particularly other mothers – will understand how you feel, even if they have not felt the same way themselves. We have all heard of cases of post-natal depression so no one will disbelieve you and most people will genuinely want to help you.

You could talk to your friends, members of your family or your health visitor. Or you might be happier with a professional counsellor or members of a specific support group. Whoever you chose, the sooner you start to talk about how you feel, the sooner you will be on the road to full recovery.

However house-proud you might normally be, don't worry too much about a little dust or an untidy room. It is hard enough to fit housework into the busy routine of looking after a new baby when you are feeling well and strong. If you happen to be under the weather for any reason, it is just not worth putting yourself under extra pressure either by trying to do too much or by worrying because it has not been done.

Perhaps you can find someone to help you for the first few weeks – maybe a friend or, if you can afford it, some paid help. And remember – if people come to visit, it is because they want to see you and your baby, not because they have come to inspect your polishing skills.

If you have a husband or partner, make plans in advance for him to take time off to be with you in the early days after the birth. If you are a single mother, try to arrange for a friend or a member of your family to stay with you during that time. It is only too easy to exaggerate problems so that they grow out of all proportion when you don't have another caring adult to talk to.

It is important that you eat well at this time, particularly if you are breast-feeding your baby. But there are many nutritious foods which require minimal cooking – or even none at all. Concentrate on these foods and conserve your energy for those jobs you *have* to do.

If you find yourself in a difficult financial situation, make enquiries (or have someone do so on your behalf) to see whether you are entitled to some sort of State allowance or assistance. This could help to lighten the pressures upon you and leave you free to look after yourself and the baby.

Even those suffering from severe post-natal depression usually have some days on which they feel somewhat better. It is very tempting to take advantage of such days and use them to take care of things which seem to entail too great an effort at other times. Please don't be tempted. This is not the time to worry about spring-cleaning, redecorating or planning a house move.

This is a time for you and your new baby to get to know each other and to enjoy each other.

Find a local mother and baby group and go along there (your local library or doctor's surgery should have details). Just talking to other mothers, hearing their experiences and realizing that you are not alone can make all the difference to the way you feel. And it is good to have somewhere specific to go where you know you will have something in common with the other people you meet there.

Children and stress

We live in a time when stress is on the increase at all ages – and children are not exempt from its pressures. Just as it is not possible to remove all possible causes of stress from the life of an adult, you cannot build a cage around your child to prevent stress-inducing situations occurring. But just as you can work towards making yourself more positive and more resilient, you can do the same for your child, thus ensuring that his approach to life is as positive as possible.

(If I use the term 'he' when referring to a child, please don't think that I am being politically incorrect, but it is so cumbersome to constantly write 'he or she' or 'him or her'.)

Stressed mother equals stressed child

Children are experts when it comes to picking up the atmosphere which surrounds them – and this starts at a far earlier age than you might think. From babyhood onwards, your child will sense your mood and react to it, even though he might be too young to understand the reasons for it.

If you find that your child is constantly irritable or unhappy (assuming that you have checked to ensure that there is no physical cause for this), perhaps you should look at yourself and what is going on in your own life at the moment – and how you are responding to it.

Of course there are going to be times when you are worried, angry, unhappy, etc., and I am not in favour of pretending that all is well when it is not. After all, we want our children to understand that we are human beings and that, as such, we are prey to all sorts of emotions – not all of them good ones. And provided these negative moments are counteracted by the positive ones when we are happy, optimistic, loving and caring, no harm is going to be done.

Trouble arises, however, when we find ourselves under great pressure and become stressed as a result. It is then that our children are likely to become stressed too and this can lead to all sorts of problems at home and at school. Not the least of these is that any child who realizes that there is a negative atmosphere in the home and who does not understand why this should be so is likely to think that *he* is the cause of it. The guilt and anxiety this can set up in the subconscious mind of the child is likely to plague him years later in adult life when he finds that he has little confidence and very low self-esteem.

If your child is old enough to talk to about your problems, let him know a bit about what is going on and the fact that you are worried. Naturally, you will do what you can at the same time to reassure him about the outlook for the future.

You will have to judge your words and the content of what you say according to the age and personality of the child. It will not do a teenager any harm to know as much of the situation as you wish to tell him. When it comes to a much younger child, it is probably sufficient to let him know that you have a lot on your mind at the moment and sometimes this makes you a bit irritable – emphasizing that this is not his fault and that everything will soon be all right again.

Even if you are wonderfully free from stress, it is quite possible for your child to have problems of his own. Since no mother likes to see her child unhappy, and also because these problems and his reaction to them will eventually put pressure on you, the more you can do to help him overcome them, the better it is for both of you.

Identifying stress in your child

Most adults will tell you when something is wrong, but children are not always able to do so. It is, therefore, up to you to be on the lookout for signs and symptoms of undue stress. Some of the most common changes in behaviour are:

Aggression

A baby may have no other means of expressing his frustration than to scream or cry, but aggressive behaviour in an older child can be a symptom of underlying stress.

If your child suddenly becomes aggressive towards other children or their possessions or if he begins to bully a particular child, you will naturally want to put an end to his antisocial behaviour – and this can be done with the right loving and caring attitude as well as firmness on your part. But it is also very important to look behind this new attitude to see if you can discover the reason for it.

If his aggression takes the form of head-banging or the infliction of injury upon himself, this can be a sign of a more deep-rooted problem and it is therefore advisable to seek professional help.

Onset of fears and phobias

It is important here to distinguish between the fears which all children experience at different stages of their lives and those which seem to occur suddenly and to create a sense of panic in the child.

Sometimes these fears will have been absorbed from the adult closest to the child without anyone having realized what was happening. If you are frightened of thunderstorms, for example, then however much you might try to disguise that fact from your child, he will subconsciously pick up the changes in your body language when one occurs. And, because to a small child, adults are always right, he will react to this by becoming frightened during thunderstorms too.

Other fears – and particularly when they reach phobia level – can be the result of stress in his life at that particular time. But the fear itself does not always reflect the actual cause of the stress. For example, it is not unusual to find a sensitive child becoming frightened of going to bed when there has been a recent bereavement in the family. Because both sleep and death result in someone lying very still with their eyes closed, the latter may trigger off a fear of the former.

Constant tearfulness

All children cry if they are hurt or unhappy, but should you find your child crying more frequently and sometimes for no apparent reason, there may well be an underlying stress-related cause. If there is, simply telling him not to cry will not be of much use – he probably cannot help doing so and possibly does not even know why he is doing so.

Bedwetting

If a child who has not previously had a problem starts to wet the bed, it is not unusual to find that he is suffering from stress. There is no point in being cross with him or punishing him; it is better to ignore the symptom – even though it does mean extra work – and concentrate on the underlying cause.

Change in eating habits

Just as in adults, a sudden change in eating habits in a child is a common indication of stress. It may be that he will find it difficult to eat – or even refuse to do so – or he might turn to food for comfort and eat non-stop.

Lying or stealing

Very young children may invent fanciful tales; older ones may lie to get themselves out of trouble – 'I didn't do it'. While such lies are to be discouraged, in themselves they are not indicative of any underlying stress in the child's life. The problem arises when they tell needless lies which serve no purpose – ones which do not help them avoid a punishment or make them seem more important.

Stealing is another indication of stress in the child's life – particularly when he has no real need or desire for the items he steals.

If your child steals, you must confront him with it – but only if you are *absolutely certain* of your facts. Nothing is more hurtful than unjust accusation. Of course you must let him know that his behaviour is unacceptable, but it is important to reassure him at the same time that you love him very much – even if you do not approve of his current behaviour.

Common causes of stress in children

Divorce or separation

At the time of writing, each year at least 150,000 children under the age of 16 are affected by the divorce or separation of their parents. In many cases the parents themselves are going through such a difficult – and often acrimonious – period in their lives that they may fail to realize the harmful effect this is having upon their children.

Just because you never have a row in front of the children does not mean that they are not all too aware of what is going on. And what they guess or believe is happening is likely to be far worse than the reality of the situation. As a hypno-therapist and counsellor, I see many of these children years later when they consult me as adult patients. I know how distressing the silences and the whispered exchanges can be to a young child. I also know that, unless firmly and repeat-edly assured otherwise, most children assume that they are at least in part to blame for the divorce.

It is really important to let the child know what is happen-ing as soon as anything is definite. Children can cope with the reality of the situation far better than most adults realize; it is the uncertainty which causes them to become stressed. And, sad though it may be, it is a fact that almost every child these days knows of a contemporary whose parents have parted.

Whatever happens, try not to involve your child in any disputes which may occur between you and your partner. Even if you are the 'wronged' one in the relationship – and however tempting it may be to let your child know what his father has done and how greatly he has hurt you – do try and resist the temptation to critize your partner in front of the child. the resulting emotions could be too difficult for him to handle.

Steven was nine when his parents divorced. The marriage had been unhappy for some time as a result of his father's alcohol-ism. When sober, Jim was quite a reasonable man but, when drunk, he became violent and would often hit both his wife and his daughter – though he never struck Steven.

After the divorce Steven would visit his father on alternate weekends, although his sister never went. Jim never drank on these occasions and would take his son fishing or to a football match.

Steven had enough problems coming to terms with what had happened – he was aware of his father's violence towards the women in the family – but this was his daddy and, despite his faults, the little boy loved him.

The situation was difficult enough for a nine-year-old to cope with but it was made far worse by the attitude of both his parents. His father would complain to him about his mother, blaming her for the fact that he had lost his home and now had to live in a caravan while still paying the mortgage on the former family house. His mother – understandably – was extremely bitter about the way she and her daughter had been treated and took every opportunity to criticize Jim in front of the boy. The result was that such great stress was put upon the child that not only did his school work suffer, but he developed a nervous twitch which caused him to be mocked by the other pupils – thus making his situation worse.

However difficult it may be, for the sake of your child try to keep the atmosphere at home as harmonious as possible. The most important thing is for both parents – before the separation and afterwards – to reassure him as often as possible that, although they may no longer wish to live together, they both still love him as much as ever.

Abuse

The child may be the victim of different sorts of abuse – mental, physical or sexual – and while we would all like to think that it is only strangers who do these terrible things to our children, the fact remains that in more than 75 per cent of cases, the abuser is known to the child.

It is interesting to note that in addition to any other feelings the child may have – fear, anxiety, unhappiness – there is one emotion common to every child who has ever been abused in any way – guilt. Every child victim feels that in some way the abuse meted out to him is his fault and that he is therefore tainted, dirty and unworthy of love.

However much these feelings are suppressed during the remainder of the child's growing years – and, indeed, some children manage to completely block out the painful memories – that sense of unworthiness is imprinted firmly upon the child's subconscious and remains with him. In almost every case it will come to the fore again in adulthood and it will be necessary for the individual to seek professional help to undo the emotional harm done to him all those years earlier.

Bereavement

Any child who is aware of the death of a member of the family or a friend will, of course, feel grief and sadness – just as an adult does. This is natural and, properly handled, will pass in time.

Long-term stress is caused, however, when that grief is not properly handled and a train of wrong ideas is set in motion.

Some people talk about the person who has died as 'going away' or 'going to sleep' and these expressions can induce in the child a fear of journeys or of bedtime – either for himself or for other people he cares about. If there is talk of the deceased person 'going to Heaven' or 'going to be with God', the child could become frightened of going into a church in case he too were to die.

Some people, with the best possible motives, send their child away while all the practicalities which their religion (or lack of it) dictates should follow a death are carried out. When the child returns, it is all over and everything is back to 'normal'. Only there is someone missing – someone people are often careful not to refer to in front of the child.

Children are like adults; they need to grieve and to find their own way of saying goodbye. To deprive them of this is not being kind as it can cause many difficulties, both at the time and in the future.

Remember too that, to a child, the loss of a beloved pet can be as traumatic as the loss of a person. Children give their love unconditionally to animals as well as to people.

Problems at school

There may be many reasons why a child finds school stressful.

Little ones starting nursery school may feel insecure. *You* know when you leave him at 9am that you will be back to collect him at noon; all he knows is that his mummy is going away and leaving him with all these other people. So see if you can break him in gently by staying at least part of the time for the first few days so that he realizes that this is a fun place to be.

When he starts going to school all day, it is more important to ensure that he knows how to dress himself and go to the toilet alone than to worry about whether or not he can read and write. Having said that, you can give him a less stressful start if you have already spent time looking at books with him and giving him the tools with which to draw and colour. If he shows signs of wanting to read before starting school, by all means help him to do so – but never try to force him or lessons of any sort may become a battlefield.

Because the child now has two sets of authority figures – at school and at home – he could become distressed if there is any conflict between them. Where possible, avoid contradicting the teacher's way of doing things and remain supportive of what he is learning.

Changing schools can be stressful at any age. Suddenly you leave one set of friends behind only to enter an environment where everyone else appears to know one another and you feel the odd one out. You can help reduce this stress by contacting the school beforehand and asking whether it is possible for your child to meet another pupil of similar age before he starts there. At least he will then find one familiar face in the crowd.

Exams are stressful for anyone, at any age. A little stress at such a time is not altogether a bad thing – the extra adrenalin often helps us to think quickly. But too much can cause the opposite to happen. I have even known of pupils who, when they turn over the exam paper cannot understand the questions printed there for about ten minutes. You can help by reassuring your child that, provided he does his best, you will be proud of him – whatever the result. At the same time, try to ensure that his home life is as free as possible from stress at this time.

It is terrible to discover that your child is the victim of bullying at school – and it can be just as terrible to find that *he* is the bully.

If you discover that your child is the victim, you must report it to the school at once – even if he asks you not to. At the same time, be as loving and supportive towards him as you can. Telling him to 'stand up for himself and hit back' is not the answer – particularly if he is not aggressive by nature. But you could try and boost his confidence in other ways by encouraging him to join a club or to get to know other people away from the school environment.

If your child is the bully, you must make it clear to him that this is something you will not tolerate – but trying to give him a taste of his own medicine achieves nothing as it reinforces his belief that it is all right for the stronger to hit the weaker. Try and encourage him to see things from the point of view of his victim and, if he is old enough to understand, remind him that only the weak and insecure feel the need to inflict pain on others.

Keep lines of communication open with the school and ask to be kept informed about the situation. At the same time, ask yourself why your child feels this need to bully others. What is making him feel so insecure?

Some children have actual learning difficulties so it is advisable to keep an eye on your child's progress from the beginning so that you are aware of any problems as soon as they arise. Others, who may appear to have difficulties, can in reality be suffering from some physical defect such as poor sight or hearing. There may be evidence of dyslexia and this can now be diagnosed and helped at a very early age.

All children have some special aptitiude, though perhaps not an an academic one. Reduce your child's stress and boost his self-esteem by encouraging him to feel confident in other areas of his life.

The more you can do to reduce the stress your child feels – whatever his age – the more harmonious your home life is likely to be and the freer from stress you will remain.

Chapter Eight

Women on Their Own

There may be many reasons why a woman might find herself living alone. Sometimes this will be through choice; perhaps she has not found anyone with whom she cares to spend her life – or perhaps she has no desire ever to do so. She may have been involved in a relationship and, for any of a multitude of reasons, decided to end it and to live alone, either temporarily or permanently.

Of course she might not be alone through choice. It could be that she would dearly wish to be involved in a close, loving relationship but none has come her way; her partner might have left her or she could have been through the trauma of the death of the man she loved.

It is not my aim here to compare the relative merits of living in a partnership or living alone – each woman must make her own choice. What I would like to do is help you to make that time when you are living alone as positive and stress-free as possible. And that applies whether you are 'between relationships' – that is, hoping that you will find another chance to be happy as one of a couple – or have decided that you would prefer to remain alone for the foreseeable future.

Even if the latter is the case and you think at the moment that you would prefer – for whatever combination of reasons – not to enter into another marriage or close relationship in the future, I would urge you to face that future in an open-minded way without excluding any possibility as far as relationships are concerned. Concentrate on living your life as fully and as positively as you can and, for now, let the future take care of itself. I have known women who have insisted that they never want to marry or share their lives with a man again but who have been drawn into what turned out to be loving and caring relationships. Others who were anxious to find another partner as soon as possible have found, when this did not happen, that they actually enjoyed living alone and felt no sense of deprivation because of it.

Women who choose to live alone

This choice can be made for a number of different reasons, as the following cases illustrate.

Josie's husband died after they had been married for nearly 40 years. Once she had gone through the grieving process, Josie made a firm decision that she did not wish to marry again. Her marriage had been very happy and she had two married daughters and three lovely grandchildren. She had a part-time job which she enjoyed and, having lived in the same house for over 20 years, a wide circle of friends. She felt that no one else would be able to match up to Frank and that she would be quite content to make the most of her life as it now was, complete with many happy memories of the time they had spent together.

Suzanne was a career-woman who had reached a very high position in a large multinational organization at a very young age. She found her work – which entailed a great deal of dedication, irregular hours and frequent international travel – extremely fulfilling. Her friends were mostly people involved in the same sort of work who understood the constraints put upon social activities by the demands of the job. Although she had been involved in various short-term relationships – often based more upon physical attraction than anything else – she had always been certain that at no time did she want anything more permanent. She felt completely fulfilled by her current lifestyle and had no desire to set up home with anyone – and certainly did not want to have children.

Bridget had never been involved in a serious relationship of any sort – and felt no desire for one. Her own parents had divorced when she was just a child, her brother's wife had left him to go off with another man and her sister was just going through her second divorce. She had seen so much heartache and acrimony surrounding marriage that she preferred not to be involved in any way. She had quite a busy life, with a full-time job and various cats and dogs to care for. She was on good terms with her neighbours and was often called upon to help care for her young nieces and nephews.

Vivienne was very bitter about men. Married for the first time when she was just 19, she divorced her husband for adultery three years later. Since that time she had been married once more and had lived at different times with two other partners. In each case the relationship had deteriorated quite rapidly and the man had left Vivienne for another woman. She was convinced that no man was capable of being faithful to his partner and determined that she was not going to put herself in the position of being hurt again. So bitter was she that she found it quite difficult to be civil to men she met socially – in fact she usually went out of her way to avoid doing so.

There is a great difference in attitude between Josie and Suzanne on the one hand and Bridget and Vivienne on the other. The first two had decided, for very different reasons, that they were content to live their lives alone. This was a positive decision and – although they could not be certain what the future would hold – satisfied them at the time.

Bridget and Vivienne, however, made their decisions based on a negative attitude towards long-term commitment and the possibility of loving relationships. They were, in fact, running away from the world and denying part of their own personality. It was rather like saying 'I won't join in this game and then I can't lose' – but they were also ruling out the possibility of winning.

Yes, of course there are marriages which fail – as statistics show only too well. And of course there are men who are unfaithful to their partners (just as there are women who cheat on their men). But perhaps both Bridget and Vivienne could have looked a little more closely at their own lives and those of the people around them.

Was Bridget still allowing herself to be affected by the break-up of her parents' marriage and the distress it must have caused her as a child? Perhaps her brother and sister had been similarly affected and this had contributed to the collapse of their own marriages.

Was there something in Vivienne's attitudes or expectations within a relationship which contributed to her partners leaving her? Or was she just someone who, for whatever reason, chose the wrong partners in the first place?

Whatever the causes of Bridget and Vivienne's decisions, they were not happy women. They chose to live alone as a means of protecting themselves from possible hurt rather than because they actively wanted to be by themselves. They were thus putting themselves in a permanently stressful position.

Divorced women

I suppose it is possible to say that some women, by being the instigators, *chose* to be divorced, while others may have been unable to prevent it happening to them. But no matter who starts the proceedings involved in separation or divorce, it is an unhappy and exceedingly stressful time.

The stress in each case may be different. One woman may be dreadfully shocked to find that her partner in what she had considered to be a happy marriage had not been happy at all, had now found himself another love and wanted to be free of the marriage in order to be with her. Another may have tried for months – or even years – to make the best of a marriage which was doomed to failure. The stress in the first case would be sudden and overwhelming; in the other it would have built up gradually over a period of time. And who is to say which is the more painful or distressing?

Women may react in a number of different ways to the trauma of divorce. Some will have their confidence and self-esteem completely shattered, believing themselves to be failures who could not even maintain a successful marriage. They may feel that others will look down on them for being unable to 'keep a man'.

We all know that it takes two people to make a happy marriage and two people to create a situation where the only solution is separation. But knowing this in our heads does not necessarily make it any easier to be rational about it when the situation is going on.

It is important at times like this to talk about the way you are feeling rather than bottling it all up inside you. If you have a good friend who will listen and be understanding, so much the better. If you really feel that there is no one close enough to confide in, try and see a professional counsellor who will be able to help you.

The idea of such talk is not to convince others that it is all your fault; nor is it to heap all the blame upon your husband. The main aim is to put your feelings into words and to discuss matters with someone who, because they are not personally involved, can help you to be logical and practical about it all. Whenever something particularly stressful is going on in our lives, it is all too easy to think in circles, becoming more anxious with every passing day.

Other women may see themselves as victims and their husbands as unpleasant creatures who have behaved aggressively towards them over a long period of time. Of course, in some cases this is literally true and the woman concerned may indeed have been the victim of behaviour which was aggressive – either emotionally or physically.

Even in such cases, the woman who has the courage to say 'enough' and to leave such a marriage or relationship should be encouraged to concentrate on her bravery and her hopes for the future rather than on the fact that she put up with so much for so long.

Sometimes it is the woman who decides that, for whatever reason, she wants the marriage to end so that she can be free to live her life in the way she wants. The ending of a relationship does not necessarily imply great fault on either side.

Colleen and Ralph were married when she was 18 and he was just 19. They had known each other from the time they had both attended the same primary school. Their families were friends and it was always assumed that they would grow up to become a couple.

For the first year or two the marriage was happy enough, but as time went on and the young couple developed and matured, Colleen felt that they were pulling in different directions. Ralph was very happy with his job, his home and his young wife, while she for her part grew increasingly frustrated at the dull routine of their life. She felt that she had missed out on an essential part of her youth, not only because she had married so young but because it had always been expected that she would do so. She didn't feel that she was ready to start a family – which Ralph and both sets of parents would have loved – and wanted to know more about life and its possibilities.

It took Colleen a long time to pluck up the courage to leave Ralph. For one thing, she really cared about him (though she was not convinced that she loved him) and did not want to hurt him. For another, she did not know what it was that she wanted out of life – only that it was something more than she had. Eventually she could stand it no longer and instigated the break, but told Ralph that she would still like to be his friend. She found herself a job which would allow her time off for studying so that she could aim for higher things in the future.

After a period of time Colleen was pleased that she had found the courage to end her marriage. She was doing well in her job and she had a boyfriend whose company she found lively and stimulating. She was genuinely happy when she heard that Ralph had married again. But in the first months after leaving Ralph, she had been consumed with guilt because she knew he had been hurt. She was also frightened, not knowing whether she was doing the right thing or not. Altogether it had been a highly stressful period for her.

Even when a divorce or separation is relatively amicable and the couple have parted by mutual consent, there is still the harrowing business of telling friends and family, dividing up possessions and working out finances. If children are involved, this only adds to the stress felt by both partners – although it is usually the woman who bears the brunt of any difficulties in this area as, in the majority of cases, it is the woman who is going to have day-to-day care of the children. Just when she is feeling at a low ebb herself, she may find herself having to deal with their insecurities and problems.

If the divorce is not amicable – and even when the couple intend otherwise, this is often the case – then the stress can be even greater. Arguments over property, financial settlements and custody of the children can become heated and bitter – and, once solicitors become involved, extremely expensive. Things are said which, even if they are later regretted, cannot be unsaid and will not be forgotten.

Sometimes a woman who has been through a divorce – particularly if her husband has gone off with someone else – will be desperately anxious to find another partner as soon as possible. In part this may be to get her own back on her errant husband, but in part it will be to prove to herself that other men still find her attractive. The trouble is that when a woman is desperate for a relationship it shows, and she often finds herself attracting the wrong sort of man – one who is likely to try and take advantage of her vulnerability at such a time.

On the other hand, another woman who finds herself in the same position may deliberately reject any advances – even of friendship – from other men. She may be trying to prove to herself – or to her ex-husband – that she does not want or need a man in her life. Both these extremes can lead to stress and heartache for the women concerned.

If you find yourself in this position, the best thing to do is to concentrate on living your life for yourself – and your children if you have them. Mix with people with whom you have something in common – women as well as men – and put thoughts of the pros and cons of future relationships out of your mind. If one comes along, that is the time to decide whether it is what you want or not. Decisions made at times of great stress are unlikely to be wise ones.

Widows

To have your husband or partner die is one of the most traumatic experiences possible. Yet, as someone who has experienced both divorce and widowhood, I can understand why divorcees often feel that theirs is the greater pain. A husband who dies has not chosen to leave you while a man who divorces you has done just that.

As in the case of divorce, becoming a widow may involve a sudden shock or be a long, stressful process. Your husband could die in a motor accident or, as mine did, suffer a sudden heart attack. Or you could have nursed him through a long illness, knowing perhaps what the final outcome would be. (Even in such cases, when the death is greeted with a sense of near relief because it brings an end to pain and suffering, no one is ever really prepared for the fact of death and the pain suffered is no less great.)

The new widow finds herself surrounded by stress. She has to go through all the natural phases of the grieving process – and this includes such emotions as guilt and anger, which may well take her by surprise. She has to cope with the attitudes of other people, some of whom will be caring and supportive, allowing her to talk or cry as she wants. Others, however, probably out of embarrassment, obviously don't know what to say when they meet her and may even dodge into a shop if they see her approaching in case they say the wrong thing.

The first year can be extremely difficult as each 'special day' approaches. Birthdays, anniversaries, Valentine's Day, Christmas – all these can be stressful occasions and the widow may not know whether to try and keep things as normal as possible for the sake of children or other people, or whether she should just hide away and pretend that they are just days like any other.

There is no right or wrong answer to this. Each woman has to find her own way of coping. But I can tell you from experience that once you have dealt with each of those days once, it is never so traumatic again. You may always think of your husband on some special date but the pain really does get less as time goes on.

Living alone

Whatever your reason for being alone, whether it was your choice or not, once the situation has arisen the problems are very much the same. (For the purposes of this section, I am calling it 'living alone' even if you have children. 'Alone' refers to being without a husband or partner in your life.)

Because so many people – men and women – now live alone, there is less embarrassment and social stigma attached to this. At one time, although a single man would be welcomed, there was no place for single women at social gatherings. Perhaps, in any age when most women were married, it was assumed that any woman who did not have a partner must be on the lookout for one.

Also, because many women – married and single – now have responsible jobs which may necessitate travelling alone and eating in hotels and restaurants alone, this also is more accepted. At one time single women in hotels were very much second-class citizens. They were given tables in the darkest corner of the restaurant and were certainly not expected to enter the hotel bar alone. Hotels have now realized what valuable customers women can be and many of them cater especially for them, reserving entire floors for women guests and ensuring that they are well looked after.

So, if on the whole other people do not now look down upon single women, what is it that keeps some women tied to relationships which are making them unhappy? The answer to that is very often – fear. And yet it is far more difficult and far more stressful to live every day in a marriage or relationship which is wrong for you than it is to make it on your own.

Women who are frightened to break away from the security – as they see it – of a marriage are women who do not like or respect themselves very much. I am not criticizing them for this – in many cases this situation has arisen because of people or events in their past. Sometimes these events occurred at a time when they were far too young to realize what was happening and their negative self-image was formed before they could do anything about it.

But even if that was the situation in your case, it does not have to continue. You may not have been the cause of your poor self-esteem but you can certainly decide how you regard yourself in the future. The one thing common to every woman is that she can change herself should she wish to do so.

I am not pretending that it will always be easy. Human beings have a natural resistance to change, even when it is for their own benefit. It is often simpler to leave things as they are. What I am promising you, however, is that, should you choose to make the effort, change is possible and, once made, can be permanent. You can become the person you have always wanted to be. You may be able to do it alone or you may need some help, but one thing is certain – you can do it.

Specific problems

All women – and indeed men – face different problems at different times of their lives. But there are some situations which women who are alone often find particularly difficult. Knowing this often makes them avoid these situations altogether, but this is not the answer and can lead to them becoming reclusive and introverted.

Outings and holidays

Going out – whether for a meal, to a theatre or a cinema – is more fun when you do it in the company of someone else. And if you have just ended a marriage or relationship, it feels as though that 'someone else' ought to be a man. But why? It can be just as enjoyable when you go with a woman friend or, indeed, with a group of friends. And at least you can make certain that you are going with someone who enjoys the same sort of meal, play or film as you do. You don't have to spend an evening doing something you would rather not do just to be with your partner.

I often go to the theatre with a woman friend who is, in fact, married. Her husband does not enjoy theatre outings and the cost of seats is so high now that it seems foolish to pay the price if you are not going to get pleasure from it. This way everyone is happy – and my friend doesn't have to sit in a theatre knowing that her husband is finding the whole thing tedious and is only there to keep her company.

Daytime outings are not too difficult if you have children

– and if they are still at an age when they want to go out with their mother as opposed to their friends! But many women who are completely alone find Sundays and bank holidays long and hard to fill.

This should not prove to be such a problem in this day and age when all sorts of special interest groups exist. Whether you enjoy rambling, growing geraniums, amateur dramatics or stamp collecting, there is a group for you. Fund-raising events are often held on Sundays and bank holidays; if there is one in your neighbourhood, why not offer to help in some way. Not only would your time be filled in a positive and productive way but the spirit of camaraderie between people working for a single cause is often very great and you will soon be accepted as one of the group.

Shortly after she split up with her partner of seven years, Mary moved to a small market town in Sussex. Her immediate neighbours were friendly, though not intrusive, but she found that weekends and bank holidays were difficult times for her. Then a committee was formed to raise money to help a local hospice.

Feeling a little awkward because she did not actually know any of the committee members, Mary nevertheless offered to help in any way she could – and her offer was gratefully accepted. Soon she found herself attending meetings, making cakes and selling raffle tickets – and on friendly terms with the other people involved in the scheme.

Since many of the fund-raising events took place at weekends and on bank holidays in order to attract the maximum number of visitors, Mary now had something to occupy her at such times. Not only that, but she became friendly with another woman on the committee – a single mother whose son had just left home to go to university. The two women discovered that as well as enjoying each others company, they had several interests in common. Without actively trying, Mary now had a companion with whom she could go on outings.

When it comes to holidays, you do not have to be alone. There are various organized holidays run by companies specializing in vacations for single people, ranging from Club 18–30 at one end of the scale to SAGA at the other. If this sort of thing doesn't appeal to you, have you thought about going on a learning holiday? These can be instructive (painting or handicrafts courses) or strenuous (walking holidays or hang-gliding lessons) but can also be more serious (bridge holidays – although I have never been on one of these, I am assured by those who have that the whole thing is taken very seriously indeed).

All such holidays cater for people who are alone and because of this you might well find that you form friendships with some of your co-travellers. At least you will know that you share at least one common interest – and that is as good a basis for friendship as any.

Of course there is nothing wrong with travelling on your own. You will be able to go at your own pace and see the things you want to see, eat the meals you want to eat and stop at the places which most interest you. If you decide to try this, you will probably find – as I did when touring Ireland – that it is more fun to stay in small hotels, guest houses or bed and breakfast establishments than in the larger, more anonymous hotels. In these smaller places you soon find people to talk to, whether it is the owners or other guests.

Loneliness

At the risk of sounding heartless, loneliness is often a form of selfishness. The lonely person is concerned only with how *she* is feeling and what people are thinking about *her*. If she could only learn to set out to try and make other people feel less uncomfortable, she might well find that she forgets to be lonely at all.

I know that is an over-simplification of the situation and that a great deal of loneliness stems from a lack of confidence or poor self-esteem. I can promise you, however, that this can be turned around and – while you may never have the desire to dance on a pub table or bathe in the fountains of Trafalgar Square – you can certainly learn to be more confident in company.

Suppose you are someone who doesn't like gatherings of people because you always find yourself lost for words and unable to approach others and make conversation. Rather than avoiding such situations altogether, why not prepare for them. The next time you find yourself in a group of people, look for the person who seems to be finding it difficult to join in – and one nervous person can always recognize another. Go up to her and see what you can do to make her feel more comfortable and more at ease.

Because she may be even more nervous than you are, try starting the conversation. Before you tell me that you can never think of anything interesting to say, remember that such gatherings are places for simple social chit-chat rather than deep, meaningful discussions about how to set the world to rights.

Start with something basic and something which is personal but not intrusive. And try to make it a question rather than a statement. A question requires an answer, and if you respond to her answer, pretty soon you will find you have a conversation going. For example, you might say, 'Have you come a long way this evening?' Whether the answer is 'yes' or 'no', you can go on to ask where from and then tell her where you live and so on. Nothing wildly exciting but something which both parties can keep going and develop without experiencing a sense of panic about what to say next.

Boredom

If you are alone and bored, it is easy to fill your time with chores or sitting in front of the television. But unless either of these choices fills you with delight, you are going to end up feeling miserable and sorry for yourself.

If you work, it is also easy to tell yourself that you are too tired at the end of the day or at the weekend to do anything other than rest. But this is often a way of presenting yourself with a ready-made excuse to do nothing.

You have two choices. You can look on the hours in the day as something to be filled somehow until you can go to bed, or you can delight in the fact that now you have the opportunity to pursue any interest you might have. Whatever the interest and however skilled you might be at it, now is your chance to take it further. From crochet to potholing, from opera to sky-diving, there are classes and organizations for practically any interest you can name.

If money is tight and pursuing some interests might prove too expensive, consider other options. Swimming and drawing are inexpensive – walking is free.

Some interests are solitary ones – and there is nothing wrong with pursuing these *provided* you also take up something which involves other people. The last thing you need, if boredom is a problem for you, is to spend all your time on your own.

Making decisions

This may not be as difficult for the woman who has always been alone as for the one who has been involved in a relationship – however it has ended. If you are in the latter situation you are no less capable of making a decision, but until recently all your decisions were either jointly made or involved taking another person into consideration. From the big decisions (where to live, how to manage finances) to the more trivial ones (what to have for dinner, what colour to paint the dining room) there was always someone else to discuss things with – even if agreement was not always easily reached or you ended up with a compromise because nothing suited both of you. Now, suddenly, it is all down to *you* – and the responsibility may seem enormous.

There are four basic stages to making a decision and they can be applied to almost any situation you can think of.

1 Identify your needs – what is the decision which must be made?
2 Make a list of all your options – how much money is there in the bank or what food do you have in the freezer?
3 Now list all the possible solutions to your problem, including those you like and those that appeal to you less.
4 From the list above, make your choice.

Try it now. Select any area of your life where a decision has to be made and go through the process above. It works.

New relationships

Women vary in how quickly they want to become involved in a new relationship – just as their reasons also vary. One widow might have been so happy in her marriage that she can't wait to enter another to find happiness again; another might feel that since nothing could compare to the relationship she had with her late husband, she would rather be on her own than settle for second best.

Some single women are happy to remain so while others feel incomplete unless they are in a steady relationship. No one is right and no one is wrong – how you feel depends entirely upon your personality and on the relationships you have had until this point in your life.

Suppose you have decided that you are happier in a marriage or relationship than when you are not. What can you do about it? If you are past the age for discos and are not particularly keen on pubs – what do you do?

There are various ways of actively seeking a male companion – from 'lonely hearts' columns in newspapers to dating agencies or singles clubs. And it is true that some women have met the man who was to be their future partner in this way. But many more have been disappointed.

If you think about it, this is not surprising because you are meeting someone under artificial conditions. Instead of getting to know each other as individuals, from the very first meeting each of you is looking at the other as possible partnership material. This is not how it works in real life. If you have had relationships in the past, think back to how they began. In most cases the man was someone you got to know on a casual basis first – perhaps through work or college; perhaps you lived in the same neighbourhood or had a mutual friend. Any thoughts of romance, marriage or living together probably came later. So by all means try singles clubs or dating agencies, but look on them more as opportunities to extend your group of friends and acquaintances than as places to find true love. Then, if it does come along, that would be an added bonus.

So where do you go and what do you do? I think the most important thing when you find yourself alone is to set about extending your circle of friends and acquaintances of both sexes. You can do this by following your own interests – attending an evening class, becoming a member of an association or club or offering your services to a cause in which you believe. Any of these will lead you to meet people with whom you already have at least one thing in common so there should be no difficulty in breaking the ice.

As I sit here now, I can think of various friends and patients who have met their current partners in this way. One couple met while working on local hospital radio; another while learning Italian at evening school; a third at a poetry society meeting and a fourth helping to clear ditches with a conservation group.

You are bound to have something which interests you or something you have always wanted to know more about – use this as a basis for your plans and get out there and get to know people.

If you have been on your own for some time, you may find it difficult to be relaxed and comfortable when a new relationship presents itself. This applies whether you have never had a long-term partner, are divorced or have been widowed. Quite often your confidence will be at a low ebb and you may feel self-conscious and uneasy with the new man in your life.

There are a few things to bear in mind here.

Unless you are dating a 15-year-old, it is likely that the man in your life has been through at least one difficult relationship too. He may feel just as uneasy as you do.

Be honest. Tell him how you feel and why. If he is not sensitive enough to be understanding about this, he is not the sort of man you are likely to want to be with anyway.

Allow things to progress at a speed which is comfortable for you. Ignore all the claims in the media about women flinging themselves into intense physical relationships after one meeting. Of course there are some people to whom this applies – but not nearly as many as some articles would have us believe. And if it is not your nature to behave in that way, you will never be happy trying to force yourself to do so.

The positive aspects

You are a very special person; there is no one in the world quite like you. It is important that you come to see yourself in that way – as a worthwhile individual in your own right and not as someone who only functions well as part of a couple. Indeed, as has been said, if you do not value yourself, no one else is likely to do so.

Take a break here and list all your positive attributes – from kindness to reliability, from being a good listener to having a great sense of humour. (No one is trying to pretend that you don't have some negative points too – we all do – but it is important to concentrate on those which are positive.)

Look at that list. If you saw it written about someone else, you would probably think they were quite a nice person. So give yourself the credit for being a nice person too. (You're probably even better than you think – I bet you've left a lot of your good points off that list.)

Learning to think positively about yourself and improving your self-image is important – but do it for *yourself* rather than because you are trying to attract another partner. The more you like yourself, the more at ease you will be with anyone you meet – man or woman.

One of the joys of living alone is that, within the constraints of job or family, you can do what you want when you want. If you want to go for a long walk you can do so – but if you fancy spending the evening sitting in front of the television set you can do that too. If you are hungry you can eat, but if you are not, you don't have to go to the effort of either making a meal or feeling obliged to eat one that someone else has prepared for you. You can decorate your home the way you like, see the films you choose, go on the holidays you prefer . . . and so much more.

While you are in the mood for making lists, why not make another one detailing all the good things about living alone. Now you have two lists to concentrate on and between them they let you know that you are a nice person who is able to do what she wants in the day-to-day living of her life. Many people would be happy to be able to say that.

Having made your second list, you might find that the pattern of your life does not allow you sufficient contact with other people and that this adds to your sense of isolation. If this is the case, then the only thing to do is to change part of that pattern. I realize that this is not always easy – we are great creatures of habit and it is more comfortable to cling to what we know than to make changes. But, as the saying goes, 'If you do what you've always done, you'll get what you've always got.' Bearing that in mind, if you are not happy with what you've always got, it is worth making the effort to change what you do.

A positive person is willing to take chances in life. I'm not asking you to do anything dangerous, but try joining that group, going on that outing, accepting that invitation – even though there is a possibility that you will be disappointed if it does not live up to expectations. There is also the possibility that you will have a wonderful time and meet some new friends. So take the chance. What is the worst that can happen? You might have a dull time with a group of uninteresting people – but you wouldn't necessarily have had much fun sitting at home by yourself, would you?

Whether you are someone who is alone by choice or not, make the most of the positive aspects of the situation. Even if you hope that it will not last for too long and that you will soon meet a future partner, it will help you to enjoy the here and now.

Chapter Nine

The Carer

The most recent figures available indicate that there are over 6 million unpaid and non-professional carers at present in Britain. Although, of course, some of these are men, it is estimated that over 80 per cent are women. Some of these women are caring for husbands, some for parents or other elderly relatives and some for children.

The Problems

Although the day-to-day situations of these carers may differ in many ways, they have many, many problems in common. Caring on a permanent basis for someone who is unable to do a great deal for themselves is a 24-hour job and can cause the carer to feel that she is a virtual prisoner in her own home. Money, even with such assistance as invalidity benefit, is often in short supply as the carer is unable to work and earn because of her full-time duties at home. Expenses are necessarily high with the patient often requiring special foods or extra heating.

There is often very little outside help – either physically or financially. What is available varies from one county to another so it is impossible to be specific about what help can be obtained. A fact common to all counties, however, is that they now find themselves with increased demand and reduced budgets. The amount of help they can give is therefore considerably reduced.

There are often no holidays for carers; it is even difficult to arrange a short break. One woman I spoke to said that she just longed to go to the hairdresser or the library without looking at her watch and wondering what was happening at home.

Olive's husband was a chronic invalid – and had been for some years. Recurrent heart trouble had left him in a weakened state. He had difficulty in breathing and this was made worse by the panic attacks from which he also suffered.

Because of all this, Olive had become a virtual prisoner in her own home. She never went anywhere unless it was absolutely essential. If she did go out – perhaps to the local shop for necessities – she would have to spend half an hour explaining to her husband exactly where she was going and how long she would be. She had to reassure him that all would be well and that she would come straight back. On many occasions she also had to give him extra medication to calm him sufficiently for her to go out at all.

Once out of the house, she would practically run to the shop, buy what they needed and run home again. She was conscious of every moment spent away from the house, knowing that her husband would be fretting until her return. She didn't have time to choose her purchases carefully, to look at any new products – or even to acknowledge with more than a quick nod the greeting of any neighbours she might encounter.

Olive didn't blame her husband for the way he was or for the demands he put upon her. He had been close to death on several occasions and she knew that he was frightened of being alone in case he could not breathe. But she was tired – physically tired, mentally exhausted and emotionally drained.

Some carers look after their charges because they feel a deep love for them and want to help all they can. Others do so out of a sense of duty; this is their husband/mother/father/brother and they choose to take care of them because they truly believe that this is the right thing to do.

But however much they may love the person they are caring for, there are times when it is almost impossible to experience that emotion. Their patients might be difficult in so many ways: possibly they are unable to understand what is being said; they may be deliberately cantankerous, scheming and manipulative or vague and unresponsive; and no doubt they are suffering from distress as they realize what is happening to them. Their behaviour may well be caused by the condition from which they are suffering. Although the carer may be aware of this, it doesn't make it any easier to deal with such attitudes when they last day in and day out, day after day, night after endless night.

Sometimes the person being cared for realizes all too well the strain being put upon the carer and goes out of his way not to 'be a burden'. But not everyone was nice to begin with and the person who has always been a bitter and spiteful individual is not suddenly going to become a delightful person just because he is now dependent on someone else. In fact, this might make him all the more resentful, making it even harder for the person caring for him. In such circumstances it must be extremely difficult, for the carer to remain kind and pleasant at all times – and of course she doesn't. But, if she does ever shout or get upset with her charge, she usually feels dreadful pangs of guilt afterwards and this only adds to the problems she is already encountering.

> One woman, whose mother was becoming senile as well as infirm, told me how the old lady would call out to her at any hour of the day or night – although when she went into her room she had forgotten what she wanted. So exhausted was the daughter that sometimes she would lie in bed and pretend not to hear when her mother called. But then she would feel wicked and guilty for acting in this way towards the mother she had always loved.

The physical aspect

Caring for another person on a full-time basis can be very hard physically – and many carers are no longer young themselves and may have their own health problems to contend with. Lifting or bathing somebody who is not able to help themselves can put great physical strain on the body. Every year we hear of young, fit nurses who have to retire or take on light duties because of back trouble caused by lifting a patient awkwardly.

Lack of sleep is another contributory factor to the exhaustion experienced by many carers. Depending on the problem, their charge may be hyperactive, have no concept of time, have difficulty sleeping or require medication at frequent intervals day and night. The carer, particularly if taking sole charge of the person concerned, will have to adapt to this routine, however difficult it may be and however different it is to what they would have wished.

The mental aspect

Caring is a solitary business. Often there is no one at all to talk to – let alone someone who will listen and understand. Any mother at home with small children will know that – however much you love them – their conversation is somewhat limited. But when you have small children, at least you can go out and see other mothers – and you do know that they are going to grow up and go to school, leaving you some time to be yourself and to enjoy the stimulating conversation of other adults.

If you are a full-time carer you do not have this to look forward to. You could be in the same situation for years to come, with no end in sight. (And if you did allow yourself to contemplate an end, that would only cause you to suffer from even more guilt, thereby increasing your stress.)

The emotional aspect

Stress and exhaustion can lead to emotional problems. You might find yourself becoming anxious and worried or you could develop a tendency to burst into tears. Frustration with your situation could cause you to become bad-tempered with the person you are caring for, or bitter because he seems to have robbed you of your own life. Although such feelings may be short-lived, they will probably make you feel guilty for having experienced them in the first place.

And then there are the other, ongoing emotions. To watch someone you love suffering in any way is a dreadful experience and naturally makes you feel sad on his behalf. To realize that he knows precisely what is happening to him is even worse. If it were a temporary phase, at least you would be able to reassure him honestly that things would soon improve. But for most carers and their patients there is no end in sight.

It is also quite normal to feel angry – angry at life for being so unfair to the person you are caring for, angry at the medical profession for being unable to help him, or angry on your own behalf for being trapped in this situation. It doesn't matter whether the anger is based on logic or not; it exists, and it is far better to acknowledge it and to understand it than to try and deny it to yourself because you believe it is something you should not feel.

The Positive side

Until now we have been concentrating on the negative aspects of being a carer – but there is a more positive side too.

Here are just a few of the positive things I have been told by women who are long-term carers.

'It gives us time to grow really close.' This was said by a young woman whose husband had been very badly injured in a road accident. He had a high degree of paralysis accompanied by breathing difficulties, but his mental faculties were unimpaired. Initially – and quite understandably – the young man had been angry at life for dealing him this blow and had found it hard to come to terms with his condition, often taking his frustration out on his wife.

As time went on, however, he determined to improve in whatever way he could and had surprised his doctors with his determination. Confined to a wheelchair, he had learned to operate a computer using a slim rod in his mouth, and had taken up painting, using a similar technique.

For her part, his wife was inspired by his positive outlook and his will to improve. She cherished the hours they spent together, talking about every subject under the sun. Although she was oftern tired, she cared for him willingly and lovingly and they grew closer and closer.

'I get so much in return.' This was the comment of the mother of a mentally handicapped little girl who was nonetheless a delightful child. She was always laughing, always happy and always demonstratively loving. On those occasions when her mother felt tired or low, the child seemed to recognize the situation instinctively and would come to her with kisses and cuddles, offering to share a favourite toy.

'I have the chance to give back some of what was given to me.' A woman in her sixties was speaking of her elderly parents for whom she lovingly cared. This woman told me of her happy childhood, rich not in money but in love and togetherness. She felt that it was not a duty but a privilege to take care now of the mother and father who had taken care of her so well all those years ago.

So there are some positive aspects of being a full-time carer – but they are so often overshadowed by the negative ones.

Barbara had taken early retirement in order to look after her father who had become a chronic invalid and was now in the later stages of senility. She felt that the father she had always loved had disappeared, leaving this stranger she did not recognize living in a crumbling shell of a body. To make matters worse, the old man had become increasingly difficult as time went on. He became bad-tempered and verbally abusive towards his daughter and anyone else who happened to visit – although, because of his attitude, visitors were becoming rare.

Barbara understood that he could not help the way he was acting – it was all part of his illness – but understanding did not necessarily make it easier to bear. Sometimes she would lose her temper and shout at her father – and then would immediately feel guilty.

Because she was the only child, divorced with no children of her own, she felt completely isolated. She had lost contact with former friends and colleagues at the office and was only on 'good morning' terms with the neighbours – she had no one to talk to except this old man who usually did not understand what she was trying to say.

Exhausted and finding it more and more difficult to cope, Barbara knew that the time would come when it would all be too much for her and her father would have to go into a home. Because of his mental state, he probably would not have been aware of what was happening to him, but Barbara knew that she would feel a terrible sense of guilt and failure if it were ever to happen. 'Sometimes,' she told me, 'I pray that he'll die before this has to happen.'

Denise has a different problem. She is married with three young children, one of whom is severely handicapped, both mentally and physically. Her husband is as supportive as possible and they manage quite well financially, but his work takes him away from home for days at a time and the burden of caring for their son falls mainly on the shoulders of Denise.

For the moment life is not too bad. The other two children are at school and although caring for Seth is tiring and time-consuming, Denise is young and strong and loves the little boy very much.

But she worries. She worries about the effect of Seth's situation upon the other children. They never complain and they love the little boy but Denise is aware that their lives are different to those of their schoolfriends. It is more difficult to arrange for them to have friends in to play because she never knows whether it will be one of Seth's good or bad days. They cannot go on holidays like other families and even their few attempts at self-catering holidays have proved unsatisfactory because Seth becomes distressed at any break from his familiar routine. Even outings to a cinema or pizza restaurant have to be taken with one parent or the other, never as a complete family.

The other great worry for Denise concerns what will happen to Seth when she is no longer around to look after him. It would not be fair to insist that either his brother or sister promise to take care of him for the rest of his life as they will have their own lives to live. If he were to be institutionalized she knew that he would become disorientated and distressed. What was she to do?

Now, of course, it is possible that neither of these problems would arise. Perhaps either his brother or sister would willingly undertake to look after Seth; perhaps Denise would be strong enough and fit enough to take care of her son for the rest of his life. But when you are tired and anxious it is easy to see only the gloomier prospects and for these to play on your mind.

Self-help

If you are a full-time carer, there is little you can do to prevent yourself feeling stressed because there is probably little you can do to change the situation which exists. Bearing that in mind, there are still areas where you can help yourself so that you do not fall victim to any of the conditions which can result from excess stress.

Financial help

Although funds in many areas have been reduced, at the time of writing in the UK, for instance, there are still State benefits available and you should not hesitate to apply for any to which you might be entitled. This is not charity money; this is an entitlement to help you deal with a difficult financial situation.

You may find that your patient – or you on his or her behalf – can receive invalid care allowance, attendance allowance, mobility allowance or income support. The actual amounts given often vary according to area, to needs and to financial status, but it is certainly worth enquiring to see what you are entitled to. Your local reference library, Citizens' Advice Bureau and Department of Social Services should be able to give you help and information.

Practical help

There are various aids available to help those who are unable to manage for themselves – and thereby to help those who care for them. Some of these may be suitable for the person you are looking after. Whether it is a simple gadget to help pick up things without moving from chair or bed, handrails and seats to make bathing or showering less difficult, or walking frames and ramps to ease mobility, they are usually available on permanent loan from local Social Services departments or through the local occupational therapist with whom your doctor or hospital can put you in contact.

If your patient suffers from a particular condition, it is also worth contacting any support group – national or local – specifically set up to help those with that condition. They will often be able to give you practical advice and they may have details of aids which may not be generally known about. Anything which can ease the life of the person you are looking after – and therefore your life too – must be of benefit. And in many cases supply and installation are free, with the proviso that the aids are returned once the patient no longer has need of them.

Taking breaks

This is one of the most important things for a carer to do – and yet it is probably the most difficult to arrange.

However much you love the person you are caring for and however willingly you undertake the tasks required, there will be times when you feel as though you are a prisoner, trapped within four walls with a person who may not be able to communicate well with you. Apart from the fact that this is not good for either of you, it can lead you to become so frustrated with your daily life that you become angry and take that anger out on the patient.

It is not selfish to consider your own needs in this way. Not only do you deserve to have a break now and then, but in doing so you will be in a much better position to cope with your tasks when you come back. If your charge really cannot be left, even for a short period, perhaps you could approach a friend or relative who could be in the home while you take a much needed break.

One of the problems with this can be that the patient does not want somebody else there – only you. In that case, try and approach the solution gradually. Perhaps a friend could come just for ten minutes while you went for a short walk or to a local shop. Once the patient has grown used to that person, you might be able to extend your free time to an hour, or even more, to give you time to go somewhere you really want to go, to see other people and to feel that you are a person in your own right again.

There is an excellent national organization in the UK called Crossroads which provides trained relief carers for short periods. Most of these carers are former nurses or people who have worked in some other aspect of the caring professions. The service is free and there are many local branches. For details of your nearest branch, contact their head office (*see* Useful Addresses section). It is also worth approaching your local reference library who might know of similar services in your area.

Taking a longer break can often prove more difficult, but there are still ways in which this can sometimes be arranged. In some cases hospitals will admit patients for a week or two so that the carer can take a holiday – or even a complete rest at home – secure in the knowledge that her charge is being properly cared for.

If a patient suffers from a particular condition, the organization connected with that condition may well have details about relief carers, special holidays, etc. It is certainly worth approaching them for advice.

If taking breaks – short or long – is imperative if you are to remain strong enough to cope with the demands of your life, it is also vital that you find some time for yourself on a daily basis. You may be able to snatch only the occasional half an hour when your patient is asleep, but even that is better than nothing.

When you are able to take some time for yourself, make sure you spend it doing something you really want to do. Forget the chores – they will still be there later on. Spend the time being as active or idle as you wish; read a book, potter in the garden, listen to some music – or do absolutely nothing.

Joining a group

One of the worst aspects of being a full-time carer is the sense of isolation experienced. If you join a group – either an official one linked with a specific medical condition or a local self-help organization – you will go a long way towards eliminating that feeling of being alone.

If you can go to meetings and talk to other people who are in the same boat as yourself, so much the better. But even if this proves impossible on a regular basis, it does help to know that they are out there. And most support groups have newsletters or telephone helplines to help you maintain the contact which can be so necessary to your own sense of wellbeing.

Chapter Ten

Minimizing the Effects of Stress

Throughout this book so far we have looked at various situations which are specific to women and which are responsible for placing them under a great deal of excess stress. And although suggestions have been offered which are designed to reduce the amount of that stress, we all know that in many cases the circumstances are such that nothing is going to eradicate it completely.

Keeping that in mind, this chapter is designed to help you minimize the effects of that excess stress so that it does not cause you great suffering – mentally, physically or emotionally. However traumatic a situation you find yourself in – temporarily or seemingly permanently – if you can follow the stress-proofing lifestyle set out here, you will be far better equipped to cope with it.

How vulnerable are you?

Let's look first at the type of woman who is most likely to suffer from the negative effects of excess stress. Study the list of statements below and note how many of them might apply to you.

- I always like to be doing something and feel guilty if I just sit and do nothing.

- I like to keep everything in an ordered and tidy fashion.
- If I do something, I like to do it really well.
- I find it difficult to give or receive criticism.
- I dislike any interruptions of my regular routine.
- It is very difficult for me to say 'no' when asked to do something.
- I am a single-minded type of person.
- I am upset by disagreements with other people.
- I get bored easily.
- I usually put other people before myself.
- I am angry with myself when I think of my imperfections.
- I have little opportunity for privacy in my life.
- I become agitated if things go wrong.
- I have difficulty in expressing emotions or displaying affection.
- I worry just as much about small problems as I do about larger ones.

If you can answer 'yes' to six or more of those statements, then you come into the category of person who is most likely to suffer harmful effects when put under stress. For you it is really important to put into action some of the stress-proofing techniques given in this chapter.

Because each woman has a different lifestyle, no one individual is going to be able to follow all the guidelines given here. So read through them, try as many of them as possible and then select the ones which most appeal to you and which fit in most easily with your life.

If you do nothing else, I would urge you to practise the relaxation technique described in Chapter One. It need take no more than ten minutes of your day. It would definitely be a highly beneficial ten minutes – and it is not an exaggeration to say that, for some of you, it could save your life. The harmful effects of excess stress are responsible for great numbers of strokes and heart attacks, any of which would be devastating and some of which would be fatal.

If you want to make that relaxation even more beneficial, you could combine it with a visualization. All this means is that, while relaxing, you fill your mind with pictures which are pleasing to you. If you have lost the habit of using your imagination in this way, take heart because – like any neglected muscle – the more you use it, the more efficient it becomes.

At the end of this chapter you will find details of how to compose an appropriate visualization for yourself as well as a sample script for you to use or adapt. You can use this script as guidance, you can have someone else read it out to you or you can record it onto an audio cassette so that you can play it back while you follow the instructions.

Practical lifestyle changes

Delegate

Before you say that there is no task you can hand over to someone else – or that you don't know any suitable person who could take over some of your tasks and relieve the pressure you are experiencing – stop and think.

What would happen if, for some reason, you were physically unable to carry on doing all that you presently do? Suppose you broke an arm or a leg – all human life would not come to an end. Somehow or other you would have to find a way to cope and you would have to find someone to help you do it.

That 'someone' could be a member of your own family or it could be an outsider whom you have to pay. If you are a single parent trying to hold down a job while bringing up your family, are the children doing enough to help you? Even little children can be given simple tasks to do – and they often enjoy the responsibility and the knowledge that they are contributing to the running of the home. If you are trying to work and run a home too, would it be possible to pay someone to do some of the housework or gardening for you? I know this is an extra expense but the fact that you are not so stressed or exhausted will probably make you far more efficient at work. And if you became ill through stress and had to take time off work, it might cost you far more.

What is really important?

You are the only one who can decide what is really important to you where your home and family are concerned. If you are basically a tidy-minded person, living in absolute clutter can be extremely stressful. But wearing yourself out by trying to achieve impossible standards can be just as stressful – especially if it causes friction between you and other members of the family.

Decide what you will settle for, even if this involves a compromise. In one household I know of, the mother insisted that the lounge was always kept reasonably tidy and that the children had to remove their clutter when they went to bed at night. In return, she did not keep on at them about tidying their bedrooms; in fact she only went into them once a week when clean sheets were needed. She closed her eyes to the inevitable mess, insisting only that clothes for washing were put in the laundry basket and dirty mugs and plates in the kitchen.

Probably the thing which should matter most is that you and other people you care about make time for each other. Whether we are talking about partners, parents, children or friends, it is all too easy for people to get out of the habit of really talking and listening to each other. Meals taken in front of the television, people rushing off to fulfil the demands of their busy lives, everyone so exhausted by the end of the day that they can hardly speak – these are the things which can destroy the fabric of family life.

Make time for yourself

If it is important to make time for other people, it is just as important to ensure that you have some time to be alone too. Each of us deserves – and needs – an oasis of privacy from time to time, but many women feel guilty when they want to be by themselves.

If you have never before taken time for yourself and you want to avoid any misunderstandings, perhaps you could explain – to your partner, children or whoever else is involved – that by wanting some time alone you are not saying that you do not enjoy being with them. It doesn't matter what you do with your time – whether you are active or quiet – as long as you spend it doing something you enjoy and you do it for no other reason than that you want to. Of course, if you share your life with others, you should be prepared to allow them their own time too.

Watch the finances

It is perfectly natural to want bigger or better things for yourself and your family – and, of course, advertising does a great deal to encourage such desires. But if acquiring these things puts too great a financial strain upon you, the stress which will be caused can be so great that the pleasure obtained from the goods themselves will be nullified.

Most of us have financial problems from time to time and the more we can do to reduce these the better. It is well known that financial worries can lead to stress-induced conditions such as high blood pressure and even heart attacks – and we have all read reports of people who have gone to the extreme of committing suicide because of the financial quagmire in which they found themselves.

Do you always wait to pay a bill until you receive the one in bright red print – even if you have the money in your account when the original one comes? If so, have you ever forgotten to pay it on time or felt anxious in case it does not reach its destination before some essential service is cut off? I wonder whether the few pennies you might be saving in interest by keeping the money in your own account for that little bit longer is worth the added stress.

Decide whether you are the kind of person who feels happiest paying a bill in full when it arrives or whether you prefer to pay by instalments over a period of time. The former means that you would be relatively free of ongoing debts while the latter would allow you to know exactly what was leaving your account each month. Once you have chosen your preferred method, make arrangements to use it to settle as many of your regular bills as possible.

Suppose you find yourself in deep financial difficulty – what then? The most important thing is to seek advice – don't bury your head in the sand and try to pretend the problem doesn't exist. That route leads to disaster.

Most organizations – from your building society to the Inland Revenue – are more helpful than you would expect when times are hard. The people they tend to come down heavily on are those who never tell them anything is wrong but just fall more and more behind with payments.

Caroline was self-employed and although she never earned a fantastic amount, it was always sufficient to pay her bills and give her a reasonable lifestyle. In the early 1980s she had one exceptionally good year, but this was followed by two very bad ones as the recession began to bite.

Because at that time income tax was paid on previous earnings, during one of these very bad years Caroline suddenly received a demand for a far greater amount than usual – and she just did not have it. Her initial reaction was to panic, but then she decided that the only thing to do was to explain the situation to her local tax officer.

Waiting for the date of the appointment, Caroline grew increasingly anxious. She had nightmares about finding herself homeless or having to close her business. When the meeting actually took place, she told the tax inspector the truth – she did indeed owe the amount demanded but she just did not have it.

To Caroline's surprise the tax inspector was very understanding and they agreed upon a fixed monthly amount that she would pay until business picked up again. Seeing Caroline's amazement, the inspector explained that the people they were worried about were those who ignored demands or tried to evade paying tax altogether. They were always willing to make specific arrangements with people who contacted them and explained their situation.

Take a break

Not everyone wants – or can afford – a fortnight's holiday in the summer. But that doesn't mean that you shouldn't try to have a change from your normal daily routine. If you have a job, make sure you take your holiday allowance whether you actually go away or not. If you do not work outside the home, try to have a complete break in routine every now and then.

Some people prefer lots of individual days off, some like long weekends at intervals throughout the year, while others take so long to unwind that unless they have a holiday of at least 10 to 14 days they don't really feel any benefit at all. Decide which are the best sort of breaks for you – and then make sure that you have them.

Holidays don't have to be expensive. You don't have to spend a fortnight on a luxury cruiseship – wonderful as it might be. Individual days out can be great fun, relaxing and leave you feeling refreshed and ready to start again. There are, however, certain criteria to bear in mind.

Aim for a change of scene where possible as it can stimulate the imagination and bring great pleasure.

Try to avoid being contactable; only tell people where you are going if you know they are not going to call on you when they have problems. If you must take a mobile phone, keep it switched off so that it is available for use in an emergency but other people cannot get hold of you – unless you want them to.

Make sure the break involves doing something you want to do. There is no point spending two weeks on a beach if you hate sun, sand and sea. Aim to spend time doing things you enjoy with people you care about. If you have a family, this may involve a certain amount of compromise – 'we'll go to the beach in the morning and sight-seeing in the afternoon', or 'you go out on the boat while I wander round the market and we'll meet for lunch'.

If you decide not to go away but to spend your holiday at home, make sure that you don't just use the time to catch up on chores or prepare for when you go back to work. Be self-indulgent and read that new novel, visit your friends or take a day-trip to a place of interest. That way your holiday will still relax and refresh you.

Mini-breaks during the day are also important when it comes to reducing stress. If you are someone who usually grabs a piece of toast while rushing round the house in the morning or thinks that lunch is a bun to be eaten at your desk while finishing that piece of work, you are greatly increasing the amount of stress in your life.

Perhaps by getting things ready the night before you will find time to sit and eat that toast in a more relaxed way; this will give you a much less stressed start to the day. As for eating at your desk, did you know that the human brain only works to optimum capacity for up to 75 minutes or so? So you are probably not achieving a great deal while forcing yourself to stay at your desk during lunchtime.

Get up a little earlier

I can almost hear the groans as you read those words, but an extra half hour at the start of the day can make all the difference when it comes to stress. You will be able to take things a little more slowly, to talk to your family, to cope with all those last-minute crises which often arise even in the best-regulated households.

Try it. Just for two weeks try getting up half an hour before your normal time every single day (well, all right, you can have Sundays off) and see whether the more relaxed start to the day makes it all worth while.

Remember your friends

How often, when Christmas comes around, do we realize that we are writing cards to people with whom we haven't been in contact since December last year? Life today seems to be lived at such a hectic pace that there is little time left for contact with friends. But if we allow this to happen, we are in danger of losing so much.

The people we care about – whether friends or family – are so important. To lose touch is a tragedy – and one which can be avoided. Aim to find time to see them – anything from a 15-minute chat over a cup of coffee to an informal supper in the kitchen.

Read through the types of change it is possible to make in your everyday life which would help to reduce the amount of stress surrounding you. Most of them are quite simple changes but the difference they can make is enormous.

Helping yourself

Relax

We have already looked at the importance of learning to relax if you are to counteract the physical effects of excess stress. A good relaxation technique need take no more than 10 or 15 minutes a day – but it does need to be done every day. Many people find they like to do it last thing at night as this usually ensures a good and refreshing night's sleep as well as a release of tension.

The one thing to remember is that however tense you may be at the minute, *everyone* is capable of learning to relax, although some may need to persevere a little more than others. In nearly 20 years of practice, I have never found anyone who, provided they are willing to keep on trying, has not been able to learn to relax within a fortnight.

Breathing

Yes, I know you have been doing this for a long time now – but have you been doing it correctly? I doubt it. Very few of us do. Breathing correctly improves your health, your looks, your energy level and your ability to think clearly.

Most people use only half their breathing potential – this means that they are expelling only half the amount of toxins they could eliminate if they breathed correctly.

There is also a strong link between breathing and the emotions. Think of anyone in a state of panic and you will know that their breathing is usually rapid and shallow, while someone who is calm and in control will be breathing more slowly and regularly. So, the next time you feel yourself beginning to be overtaken by symptoms of stress, try calming your breathing pattern until it is slow and regular in rhythm.

You could also spend a few moments each day practising the following simple breathing technique so that your mind and body grow used to the sensation of deep, relaxed breathing. This has to come from the diaphragm rather than from the upper chest which is where most of us breathe for most of the time.

1 Stand straight but not tense, feet slightly apart and facing forwards.
2 Place your hands over your ribcage so that your fingertips are just touching.
3 Breathe in from the diaphragm so that, as your ribcage expands, your fingertips are forced apart.
4 Hold that position for a count of three before breathing out again. As you expel the air, your hands should come together, fingertips touching once more.

Ideally you should practise this for at least five minutes a day. It may feel strange to you at first but don't worry – it will soon become quite natural.

Nutrition

We all know the sorts of foods which make up a healthy diet – and some of us stick to them while others do not. At those times when you are feeling fit and well and in control of your life, it doesn't really matter too much if you over-indulge from time to time, although this should never be taken to extremes.

When you are suffering from excess stress, however, you really should try to ensure that your diet is balanced and that you are getting all the required vitamins and minerals. Such a diet will not do anything about the stressful situation around you but it will make you less likely to suffer the physical effects of that stress. In addition, it is one area of your life where you can be in control – even when everything else appears to be in chaos.

It is not always easy to assess how rich your diet is in essential vitamins and minerals, even when you are doing your best. Chemicals used on the land and the length of time it takes for produce to get from grower to shop to table can make it difficult to know the value of the food you are eating. If you are suffering from a deficiency, however, you will probably be aware of one or more of the following symptoms.

- unusally dry or flaky skin;
- dull, dry hair;
- white flecks or noticeable ridges on your fingernails;
- tendency to mouth ulcers and/or bleeding gums;
- a very red tongue
- noticeably dry skin around your nose and at the corners of your mouth;
- a tendency to bruise more easily than usual;
- slow healing from minor injuries or colds;
- a reduced energy level.

If any or all of the above apply to you, take it as a sign that you need to be extra careful about your diet. There are many lists available (from doctors, pharmacists, nutritionalists and therapists) of what constitutes a healthy diet. If you find that there is any particular range of foods lacking in your normal diet – or which you absolutely loathe – it is possible to take the missing vitamins or minerals in the form of tablets.

Sleep

When we are stressed we most to be able to sleep well and soundly – but of course that is just the time when this is most difficult to achieve.

You know what happens: you go to bed, possibly physically exhausted, but your brain just won't stop working. All your anxieties are chasing each other around inside your head and the more you try to stop them, the faster they seem to go. You are desperate for sleep but you keep looking at the clock and seeing the hours of the night passing while you lie there tossing and turning. Eventually you drop into a fitful sleep in the early hours, only to be woken what seems like minutes later by the sound of the alarm telling you it is time to get up and face another day.

First, let's dispose of some of the myths to do with sleeping.

You don't have to have eight hours sleep a night. Some people do need this amount – or even more – but others manage quite happily on five or six.

The occasional bad night doesn't matter. It isn't pleasant but it will do you no harm. You only need to become concerned if you find yourself unable to sleep night after night.

The fact that you find it really difficult to get up in the morning even after eight hours of sleep isn't in itself a problem. Wait until you have been out of bed for about half an hour and see what you feel like then. If you feel awake and alert, there is nothing to worry about. If you are still weary or sluggish, then either you are not getting sufficient sleep or the sleep itself is of poor quality.

If you do have difficulty sleeping – whether this is a general pattern or a temporary one – you are going to find it far harder to cope with the symptoms of stress around you. It is important to break the pattern of sleepless nights and establish a new one where sleep comes easily and well. The following simple precautions may be helpful.

Avoid working (whether as part of your job or doing housework) right up until bedtime. Make sure that the last half hour is calm and restful and spent doing something you enjoy – reading a book or magazine, listening to music, etc. If you like to watch television before going to bed (or even in bed), try not to watch exciting adventure films or stimulating discussion programmes which make it harder for your brain to slow down.

Avoid caffeine-rich drinks late in the evening – they act as a stimulant. The same applies to alcohol. Many people think that a late-night alcoholic drink will help them to sleep – and in part this is true – but although the drink may help you *get* to sleep, it won't help you *stay* there and you will probably wake up more than once during the night. Try instead a warm, milky drink or one of the herbal teas such as chamomile.

If you like to have a bath before going to bed, don't have the water too hot or too cold – this would act as a stimulant to the body.

Try and fit some exercise into your day, even if it is nothing more than a brisk walk round the block. But don't do it just before bedtime – it might tire you out but it will also increase your heart and pulse rate and this is what you are trying to avoid.

A stuffy room will make sleeping much more difficult. Unless it is really cold or foggy, an open window will help. Make your bedroom a smoke-free zone – not only will sleep come more easily, but you are less likely to wake up with a thick head.

Try establishing a pre-bedtime routine and doing the same things in the same order each night. Your subconscious mind will soon come to associate this routine with the fact that you are going to bed and will make it easier for you to settle down and sleep.

Once in bed, practise a relaxation routine. You could try the one given in Chapter One, the one at the end of this chapter, or you may prefer to buy a ready-made cassette to help you.

Exercise

Physical exercise does not have to be exhausting; it does not have to be painful – and it certainly should not involve doing anything you hate. If you dread the thought of working out at a gym or pounding the pavements day after day – don't. But do try and find some form of regular exercise which you enjoy and which fits into your lifestyle.

The fitter you are, the more likely you are to withstand the slings and arrows of excess stress. We have already seen how important correct breathing can be when it comes to dealing with highly stressful situations – and exercise encourages you to breathe deeply from the diaphragm. In addition, your heart is more likely to work efficiently, your circulation will improve and you will generally feel better in every way.

To be beneficial, exercise should be regular and it should be controlled. There is no point in doing nothing for six days and then going out for a 20-mile run on the seventh. Twenty minutes three or four times a week will be enough to keep you relatively fit.

You might prefer to exercise alone – perhaps by walking the dog or going for a swim – or you might prefer to join a group or class. It doesn't matter which provided you enjoy yourself in the process – otherwise you will never keep it up.

There are a few points to bear in mind concerning excercise.

If you have any doubts about your general health or your ability to exercise, consult your doctor first to ensure that all is well.

Start slowly – particularly if you have not taken much exercise recently. If you are really out of condition, begin by practising a basic stretching and warming-up routine every day until you feel able to progress to something more energetic.

Avoid being too competitive while under stress. There is nothing wrong with a bit of healthy competition in life but do remember that competitiveness is stressful in itself; try and find something which you can do just for yourself and not with the aim of beating everyone else.

Visualization

Visualization is the use of the imagination combined with positive thinking. It is a sort of controlled daydream where you picture future events turning out just as you would want them to.

This is not just idle hopefulness but something far more powerful. It is used by most top sportsmen and women to great success. Look at the expression on a sprinter's face just before the start of a race – he is *seeing* himself winning. And just watch the world's leading tennis players as they talk to themselves on the court – they are combining visualization with positive affirmations.

A great deal of stress is caused by anticipation – what we think is going to happen or even what we dread happening. 'Suppose I never manage to sell my flat', 'What if I make a fool of myself at that interview?', 'I know I won't remember a thing once I'm in the exam room.' Too many people let themselves down by such negative programming because the mind is powerful enough to grasp those thoughts and keep hold of them until they become fact.

Visualization enables you to use that power of the mind in a positive way. Just like an actor rehearsing a part in a play, you can use your imagination to 'rehearse' your future.

Melanie ran a flourishing floristry business, specializing in displays for weddings, churches, banquets, and so on. In 1994 she won a local 'Businesswoman of the Year' award. Soon afterwards she was asked by a local women's organization if she would come and give them a talk and she agreed to do so.

As the time of the talk grew nearer, Melanie began to panic. She knew and loved her job and she realized it would make good business sense to give talks to potential customers. But she had not spoken in public since she was at school – and she had always made a mess of it then.

Because these past failures were uppermost in Melanie's mind, she was in fact already using viualization but in a negative way. She was actually picturing things going wrong – and had she continued to do so, they probably would have done.

I asked Melanie to tell me precisely what she feared. She was not worried about the topic – she really knew her subject. She was afraid of blushing, shaking or forgetting what she wanted to say when she stood up in front of all those people.

What Melanie had to do was to follow a particular routine every night for at least three weeks before the event. First she had to go through the relaxation technique in Chapter One. Then she had to picture the scene as it would be when she came to give her talk and visualize the whole thing happening exactly as she would like it to. She saw herself being calm yet enthusiastic as she talked to her audience about her work; she imagined the smiles and looks of approval on their faces as she spoke.

By feeding this image into her subconscious mind over a period of time, Melanie was actually persuading her subconscious that this had already happened. Your subconscious cannot tell the difference between an actual memory and a visualized imaginary event so it accepts your mental rehearsal as a memory of something that has already happened. And, of course, if it has happened once, it can happen again.

Melanie was perfect on the night and, as a result, was invited to speak to several other groups. Not only did she enjoy doing so, but it led to a significant increase in her already successful business.

In a case like Melanie's, you can be sure that proper practice of visualization will lead to success. But there are occasions when you cannot guarantee the outcome in the same way. Suppose, for example, that you have to attend an interview for a job you hope to get. You might visualize everything correctly and do everything perfectly on the day – but there might be another interviewee who just happens to have better qualifications than you and therefore gets the job. But even if you do not succeed, you will come away from that interview with greatly increased confidence and this will help you a great deal when it comes to further interviews.

Earlier in this chapter I said that relaxation could be enhanced by the use of visualization. This is possible because you can think of only one thought at a time, and by concentrating on a positive image which is pleasant to you, you cannot be thinking of all those problems which surround you in your everyday life.

There are various ways of using the following script to help yourself. You could read it and memorize it so that you can use it whenever you want. You could ask someone else to read it out to you as you practise it; or you could record it on an audio cassette and play it back to yourself at the appropriate time. There are just a few points to bear in mind.

The script is only a guide. If, when you have read it, you decide that you would prefer a different image, please substitute whatever pleases you.

Obviously you should avoid anything which would normally bother you. In other words, there is no point imagining a river if you have a phobia about water – or a cornfield if you suffer from hay fever.

Before you start to visualize always practise the relaxation technique already given. If you are making your own cassette, record the script straight after the relaxation technique.

To be beneficial, any form of relaxation – with or without visualization – *must* be practised regularly. Once or twice a week is not enough to make any difference. It need take no more than 10 or 15 minutes – and when you think that it could help you avoid such stress-induced conditions as strokes and heart attacks, I am sure you'll manage to find that small amount of time.

Script for visualization

It is a lovely day in early summer – warm but not too hot. The sun is shining in a clear blue sky and there is a gentle breeze blowing. You are strolling along a grassy bank near a gently flowing stream.

As you walk you can feel the soft grass beneath your feet and you watch the patterns of light and shade made by the sun shining through the leaves of trees. You are aware that there are other people somewhere in the distance but no one is close enough to disturb the peace you feel.

Walking along the bank, you gaze at the sparkling water. It is so clear and clean that you can see pebbles on the stream's bed and here and there a darting fish.

You come to a big old willow tree and decide to take a rest. You sit on the grass which is soft and cool and completely dry. The long, graceful branches of the willow surround you and enclose you in your own perfect world of peace.

Now you lie back on the grass beneath the willow tree and close your eyes. You can feel the soft grass beneath your body and the warmth of the filtered sunshine as it gently touches you. If you listen, you can hear the sound of birds singing and the gentle swish of the long branches of the willow as they gently stroke the surface of the stream.

Everything is calm and peaceful in your own perfect little willow world. No one else has ever been to this spot and no one but you will ever come here. But you can return to it in your imagination whenever you wish – and whenever you do, a sensation of peace and tranquillity will come over you.

Stay in this beautiful place for as long as you wish. When you are feeling relaxed and rested, you may either open your eyes or drift off into a peaceful and refreshing sleep.

Chapter Eleven

Help at Hand

Even after putting into practice as many of the stress-counteracting techniques as you can, you may still feel that you could do with some extra help. If so, this chapter will give you some ideas about professionals to consult, organizations to approach, books to read and addresses to contact.

Complementary therapy

There are many different types of complementary therapy but they all share the same principle of treating you holistically. This means that rather than trying to overcome a symptom, they work on the individual as a whole. This often involves taking into account not only your current condition and lifestyle but also your background and sometimes even the state of health of your immediate family and their background too.

The belief is that each person has their own basic energy force and provided that energy force is working efficiently, the body will be able to heal itself.

I prefer the term 'complementary therapy' to 'alternative medicine' because the latter assumes that it is in competition with, or a rival to, conventional medicine. This does not have to be so; the idea is that they can 'complement' each other. There are, of course, some people who completely renounce one form of medicine in favour of another – but this is a matter of individual choice and no practitioner should ever try to persuade anyone to do this.

Some people, particularly those to whom the concept of complementary therapy is new, are not certain how to go about finding a good and reputable practitioner. Of course, it is always possible to look at classified telephone directories or in the relevant pages of local newspapers, but we all know that it is not only the good who advertise.

The best guide must be personal recommendation by someone you know who has already benefited from consulting a particular therapist. But you might not know such a person or, even if you do, the therapy which was most appropriate for her might not be the best for you.

Although some charlatans set themselves up in practice after a minimum of training, it is unlikely that they will carry professional insurance – insurers will usually accept only those who have completed a recognized course in their particular field. So one of the things you can do when you telephone, or at your first meeting, is to ask about their insurance certificate.

The Useful Addresses section lists recognized registers for the major complementary therapies; you can contact these to find details of a suitable therapist in your area. (A stamped addressed envelope would probably be welcomed by any such organization – they are usually inundated with requests for information as more and more people turn to complementary medicine to help them overcome their problems.)

If you are unsure about which therapy to choose, you could approach one of the many multi-therapy clinics and seek advice there. But in any case, any ethical practitioner will tell you the truth if he or she feels unable to help you with your problem.

Once you think you have made your choice, contact the therapist concerned and ask if he or she would be willing for you to come and have a brief chat. Most therapists will do this without charging and even if you are with them only for about ten minutes, it should be enough time for you to find out whether this is the appropriate therapy for you and – even more importantly – whether you feel comfortable with this particular therapist.

That last point is perhaps the most significant of all. A therapist may be highly qualified and very willing to help you, but if, for whatever reason, you do not feel at ease with him or her the therapy is not going to work. Because complementary therapists need to be able to discuss many aspects of your life with you, you have to have confidence in them and there must be a rapport between you. Bear in mind, by the way, that all ethical therapists are bound by the same code of confidentiality as your general practitioner.

The fees charged by such therapists vary greatly in different places – with the major cities charging the most. In the UK it is sometimes possible to have referrals from doctors (particularly those who are fund-holding); this will enable you to have treatment on the NHS. If you have private medical insurance it is worth enquiring to see whether your particular policy also covers complementary therapy.

Let's look now at some of the major therapies and how they might be able to help you with stress.

Acupuncture

Most people have heard of acupuncture, an ancient Chinese practice. The theory is that energy paths link certain pressure points in the body and the life force – or *Chi* – travels along these paths. If there is a blockage in the energy paths, the Chi cannot travel as it should and health is affected as a result.

Some people are put off acupuncture because of a fear of needles, but those used by the acupuncturist are very thin and only lightly inserted. All you usually feel is a slight tingling sensation – not pain. Strict sterilization procedures are always followed to ensure that the needles are perfectly safe – but if this aspect worries you, ask for disposable needles to be used.

Aromatherapy

Aromatherapy is the use of essential oils derived from flowers, trees, plants, herbs and spices. These oils are usually massaged into the body by the aromatherapist and this results in minute particles being absorbed into the bloodstream. Each oil has a different therapeutic use and an experienced therapist will, after making a detailed diagnosis, make up a blend of oils especially for you.

It is also possible to buy these essential oils from reputable suppliers and you can then use them, in very small quantities, in your bath water or as a steam inhalation. If you are going to do this, however, it is best to get proper advice on which oils would be the most appropriate for you.

Homoeopathy

In homoeopathy, remedies are prescribed specifically for each individual patient. The treatment is based on the theory of 'like treating like' – which is completely different to conventional medicine. For example, if you happen to suffer from insomnia, rather than prescribing a substance designed to help you sleep, the remedy will contain the tiniest dose of a stimulating substance. The philosophy is based on the fact that the body is aware of what it is doing and that, by seemingly attempting to aggravate the condition, a self-healing process will be set in motion.

That is, however, a great over-simplification of the process and no homoeopath will prescribe for you without taking a long and extremely detailed history – often asking questions which may seem irrelevant but which do, in fact, have a vital bearing on the remedy prescribed.

Homoeopathic remedies do not cause side-effects and are not addictive – in fact they are often prescribed for babies and young children.

Hypnotherapy

Some people, having seen stage performances of hypnosis, are anxious about hypnotherapy because they feel that they will be out of control. But this is far from the truth.

Although hypnotherapy involves a state of deep relaxation, the patient is always fully aware of what is being said and cannot be made to do anything against her will. Think how you feel when you are in that 'twilight state' which comes between being awake and being asleep – warm, comfortable, safe, but still conscious – and you will have a good idea of what it feels like to be hypnotized.

The relaxation state of hypnosis is so therapeutic in itself that some people find it is all they need to counteract the stress they feel in their lives. But all properly trained hypnotherapists are counsellors too and will be able to help you deal with whatever problems surround you.

Medical herbalism (Western or Oriental)

Medical herbalism has been in use for thousands of years, particularly in China. Herbs are prescribed for specific symptoms after a detailed analysis and diagnosis. The remedies can be taken as an infusion, a tincture, a lotion, in capsule or tablet form or as a poultice, depending upon the person being treated. Oriental herbalism has been found to be particularly effective in the treatment of eczema, psoriasis and other skin conditions which are often aggravated by stress.

It is advisable to seek professional advice before taking herbs for any length of time as some can be toxic in large doses. In addition, pregnant women should use only those herbal remedies prescribed by the herbalist.

Useful Addresses

Complementary therapies

Acupuncture

Australian Traditional Medicine Society
120 Blaxland Road
Ryde, New South Wales 2112
Australia

British Acupuncture Council
Park House, 206 Latimer Road
London W10 6RE, UK

World Federation of Acupuncture Societies
42–62 Kissena Boulevard
Flushing, New York 11355, USA

Aromatherapy

Margaret Tozer
Australian School of Awareness
PO Box 187
Montrose 3765
Australia

Shirley Price Aromatherapy
Essentia House, Upper Bond Street
Hinckley, Leicestershire LE10 1RS, UK

Margot Latimer Aromatherapy
PO Box 65
Pineville, PA 18946, USA

Homoeopathy

Australian Federation of Homoeopaths
PO Box 806
Spit Junction
New South Wales 2088
Australia

British Homoeopathic Association
27a Devonshire Street
London W1N 1RJ, UK

National Center for Homoeopathy
801 North Fairfax Street, Suite 306
Alexandria, Virginia 22314–1757, USA

Hypnotherapy

Australian Society for Clinical & Experimental Hypnosis
Royal Melbourne Hospital
Royal Parade, Parkville
Victoria, Australia

Hypnotherapy Register
The Hypnothink Foundation
PO Box 66
Gloucester GL2 9YG, UK

National Council of Psychotherapists
Hypnotherapy Register
5 Kivernell Place
Milford on Sea, Hampshire SO41 0XH, UK

American Association of Professional Hypnotherapists
PO Box 29, Boones Mill
Virginia 24065, USA

Medical herbalism

National Herbalist Association of Australia
Suite 305, Smail Street
Broadway, New South Wales 2007
Australia

National Institute of Medical Herbalists
56 Longbrook Street
Exeter, Devon EX4 6AH, UK

Register of Chinese Herbal Medicine
PO Box 400
Wembley, Middx, HA9 9NZ, UK

Office of Medical Herbalism
2068 Ludwig Road
Santa Rose, California 95407, USA

Other organizations

Carers Association
Level 5, 93 York Street
Sydney, New South Wales 2000
Australia

Stillbirth Support Group
G9 Agnes Walsh House
KEMH, Bagot Road
Subiaco
Western Australia 6008
Australia

Crossroads (help for carers)
10 Regent Place
Rugby, Warwicks. CV21 2PN, UK

Foresight
28 The Paddock
Godalming, Surrey GU7 1XD, UK

The Miscarriage Association
Clayton Hospital
Northgate
Wakefield, Yorks. WF1 3JS, UK

American Association for Retired Persons
1909 K-Street NW
Washington DC, USA

Association for Post-Natal Illness
25 Jerdan Place
London SW6 1BE

For details of Ursula Markham's self-help cassettes and details of
assertiveness training courses, contact:

The Hypnothink Foundation
PO Box 66
Gloucester GL2 9YG, UK

Further reading

Bradford, Nikki, *The Well Woman's Self Help Directory*, Sidgwick & Jackson, London, 1990

Coleman, Vernon, *Overcoming Stress*, Sheldon Press, London, 1988

Kenton, Leslie, *Stress and Relaxation*, Century Hutchinson, London, 1986

Markham, Ursula, *Creating a Positive Self-Image* Element Books, Shaftesbury, 1995

Markham, Ursula, *Women and Guilt*, Element Books, Shaftesbury, 1995

Wilson, Paul, *The Calm Technique* Thorsons, London, 1985

Index